GIANT
JOURNEYS:

BECOMING AN IRONMAN

Doug C. W. Thomas

Hebrews 12; 1-2

GIANT

JOURNEYS:

BECOMING AN IRONMAN

DOUGLAS W. THOMSON

Kenwood Publishing Group
www.kenwoodpublishinggroup.com
Cincinnati, Ohio
Copyright © 2015 by Douglas W. Thomson
All rights reserved. Published by Kenwood Publishing Group.

ISBN-10: 0-9908682-2-2
ISBN-13: 978-0-9908682-2-4

To Stu Mills—the brother I never had, whose undaunted courage and contagious optimism provide a lifetime of inspiration.

ACKNOWLEDGEMENTS

I would like to thank my beloved wife, Gretchen, for supporting me through this endeavor. She had to endure nearly a year of my training, during which I was gone most weekends on a long bike ride or run. At the conclusion, I was often too exhausted to be of much help to her during the remainder of the weekend. Following the Ironman, I had a different focus in writing this book, but it was a time-consuming endeavor nevertheless. Her support to pursue this dream means more than she can imagine.

Again, I want to acknowledge the support of Stu, who provided the inspiration for my training and words of encouragement during a critical moment in the race. I want to thank my daughter for running with me during the last mile. That was a special time that is embedded in my memory.

I want to thank the staff of Matthew 25: Ministries for encouraging me to write about the race. Karen Otto, Joodi Archer, Katie Hallum, and Tim Mettey provided valuable suggestions for making this work flow. And I want to thank Lauren Fogle for the cover design. They are a remarkably talented team who is impacting the world. I also want to acknowledge Rev. Wendell Mettey, the founder and president of Matthew 25: Ministries. His vision for helping the poorest of the poor has made scripture come alive to many in the world.

PREFACE

Some stories just need to be told. The journey of my brother-in-law, Stu Mills, is one such story. Stu is the inspiration for this book, which tells the story of how he battled and survived a life-threatening illness. All who meet him are uplifted and improved by the experience. He certainly has been an inspiration to me. Despite the trials he has been through, he has a contagious optimism. Stu's journey back to health is a remarkable and giant journey. I hope that as you get to know him through these pages, you will gain an appreciation for his life.

At first glance, you may think there is not much in common between battling an illness and training for a race. In a race, you may have a bad day and not finish, but there is always another day. There will always be another event. Even though you may have invested a year of your life in training, if for some reason you cannot complete the race, life goes on. In contrast, the stakes could not be higher when fighting a life-threatening illness. If you lose, you will die. There is no tomorrow, at least not on this earth. Those are the stark options.

In training for an Ironman competition, I discovered there are certain universal and timeless lessons that can be learned, whether battling an illness or training for a race. I dedicated my race to Stu and embarked on my own year-long journey of self-discovery. This work is an amalgamation of Stu's story, my own journey and stories of other people. Some of these "others" I have met, and some I will never meet because our lives are separated by time and distance. Despite the differences in our backgrounds and life experiences, there is a common thread, a giant journey, running through each story. It is my hope that you will be encouraged by this work, and that it might give you the strength and courage to embark on a giant journey of your own.

People may wonder: Why attempt something as audacious as an Ironman at the age of 59? Why attempt to cover 140.6 miles in one day? That is far enough to go in a car, let alone trying to cover that distance by swimming, biking and running. There is no simple answer to that question. My own answer and drive came from the confluence of many different factors.

The first time I saw an Ironman competition on television, my emotions ranged from fascination to admiration and even disbelief, as the athletes staggered and crawled across the finish line at the Kona Ironman in Hawaii. I knew from experience that running a marathon was tough. I had run three marathons in my life, with the first two in my early 40s and the last when I turned 50. I could not imagine running a marathon after a 2.4-mile swim and a 112-mile bike ride. An Ironman seemed to be the ultimate physical challenge, and seeing those athletes stagger across the finish line only reinforced that impression. That day, I began to wonder if I could complete such an epic test of endurance. I wanted to find out exactly what my physical limits were. Could I achieve what these people had done? Did I have the mental toughness and discipline to complete the training and finish the race?

As I continued to contemplate this challenge, I realized that if I did not attempt the Ironman that specific year, I never would. My health was good, and I did not have any nagging or recurring injuries. I was not getting any younger, and the longer I waited, the tougher it would be for me to train and compete.

I also got a glimpse of the bookends of my own life. My dad turned ninety that year; my mother had died all too early of cancer at the age of sixty-four, after a brave seventeen-year battle. Dad had enjoyed good health until age eighty-seven, when he wrenched his back playing golf. The last time we played golf together, I remember watching him tee off. When he swung, he almost lost his balance and fell. He gave me a sheepish look as he regained his footing. We both knew that there would not be many more opportunities for us to play together. As matters turned out, we just played once more, and now his health renders him incapable of ever playing again.

Finally and most importantly, I decided to attempt an Ironman as a way of honoring my brother-in-law, Stu Mills. If there ever were a person who would be justified in shaking his fist at the sky in anger, it is Stu. Life has dealt him a tough hand to play. He contracted cancer while still in his twenties, and his odyssey to recovery has been an ordeal. His story is told in this book. Stu's example keeps me grounded and helps me remember what is truly important. I dedicated both the race and this book to him.

All proceeds from the sale of this book will be donated to Matthew 25: Ministries, which is a charity devoted to helping the poorest of the poor and disaster victims by providing food, water, clothing and other basic necessities to those in need. This ministry has been particularly active in responding to natural disasters and has been rated as one of the nation's most efficient charities. If you care to find out more about this charity, there will be a link at the end of this book.

A MOST REMARKABLE MAN

CHAPTER ONE

STU'S JOURNEY

One day, my brother-in-law Stu noticed some lumps in his lymph nodes. I happened to be visiting him the following weekend, and while we were out on a run, Stu commented that he had found these lumps. He thought they would go away, but they did not. He finally arranged an appointment with the doctor, who told him the lumps could be the residual effects of flu or mononucleosis. The doctor told Stu not to worry, but if they were not gone in ten weeks to come back and see him. Physically, Stu felt great, so at this point he was not concerned.

Hoping the lumps would go away, Stu waited sixteen weeks to return to the doctor. This time the doctor found more lumps in his arm and neck. The doctor was not alarmed, but as a precaution, he ordered tests, which ruled out mononucleosis and tropical viruses. Next, he removed the largest lump for biopsy testing. Still, at that time, Stu did not consider this to be anything serious.

Several days later, the surgeon called Stu and informed

him the biopsy showed that the lump was malignant. Stu asked him what that meant. The doctor said, "It means you have cancer." This happened about twenty weeks after Stu's first visit to the doctor. At that time, he was twenty-seven years old and his wife, Barb, was three months pregnant with their first child. Stu thought the results of the biopsy would show he had Hodgkin's disease, which is often curable. But the doctor explained that it was non-Hodgkin's lymphoma—an incurable form of cancer. He explained that this was a slow-growing form of cancer, which is why Stu had not felt any other symptoms. The average life expectancy for someone with this type of cancer is about a decade.

Stu then went to a cancer specialist, who outlined a plan of treatment. Since this particular lymphoma was a slow-moving cancer, the doctor's recommendation was to treat it as it affected Stu, which would take a couple of years. The doctor also suggested that Stu get a second opinion.

The second doctor disagreed. He said that since Stu was feeling well and the cancer was still growing, his preference would be to treat it aggressively now rather than waiting. Stu's body would be better able to handle the treatment. Stu and Barb agreed with this advice.

The treatment began with a recipe of drugs. Stu went in for treatment once a week for three weeks. He had a week off, and then the process was repeated. But further testing showed the cancer was in Stu's bone marrow. In fact, thirty-eight percent of his marrow was already affected. The cancer was then classified as stage four, which is the most serious stage of cancer. Still, Stu believed that if he did everything the doctor said, he would be fine.

Stu began a six- to eight-month cycle of chemotherapy treatment. At first he went into the sessions optimistically, but he quickly began to dread them. He felt sick and had back spasms before each round, and he started throwing up when he got to the treatment room. During this cycle, Stu's son Ben was born, which gave him even greater motivation to continue the treatments in order to get better.

Upon completion of this cycle, Stu was retested to monitor the results. His bone marrow had gone from thirty-eight percent to thirty-two percent affected. The cancer was still present, only slightly diminished. Stu could go through chemotherapy again, reduce the dosage of the treatment, or see a bone marrow transplant specialist. He decided to see the specialist. The specialist cautioned that this bone marrow transplant was a new procedure, and there was not a pool of survivors with Stu's type of cancer. Although he could not officially say it would work, he was confident enough to suggest giving it a try. Barb and Stu decided this was the right path.

It turned out that all four of Stu's brothers and sisters were a close enough match to donate bone marrow, but his twin brother, Steve, was the closest match. Steve was eager to give Stu his marrow, even though it was an extremely painful procedure. The doctors would have to go into his bone, aspirate the marrow with a syringe, and transfuse it into Stu. Steve's marrow was drawn from his hip, and since the doctors did not extract enough at that location, they took additional marrow from his sternum. After the surgery, Steve said it felt as if someone had hit him in the lower back and chest with a baseball bat.

The worst part for Stu was the day he left home for the hospital. Ben was three months old, and Stu hugged and kissed him for a long time. As they pulled out of their driveway, Stu broke down and cried harder than he ever had during his ordeal. He did not know if the procedure would be successful, and he knew this could be the last time he would hug and kiss his son. Prior to the transplant, all of Stu's bone marrow had to be destroyed by full body radiation and chemotherapy. Without bone marrow from a donor to replace the bone marrow that had been destroyed, he could not live.

The procedure started with four days of radiation, three days of chemotherapy, a day of rest, and then the transplant. Stu felt healthy going into the treatment, but by the end of the first day, he could not even walk out of the room. The chemotherapy was so aggressive that they attached a catheter to his bladder to flush water through his system. If the drugs had stayed in his system too long, they would have burned a hole through him.

Transplant day was anticlimactic for Stu. A little bag of blood with Steve's marrow cells was all they gave him through an IV. Stu could not believe he went through so much for just a little bag of blood. But that little bag of blood would save his life.

After the transplant, it was hard for Stu to continue. His energy was drained, and everything hurt. He could not eat. He had sores in his mouth. He had tubes sticking in all openings of his body. He was nauseated constantly. It was hard to breathe, and he had a fever. In this condition, he began his own desperate and giant journey toward recovery.

LOUISVILLE IRONMAN: JOYOUS SUFFERING

CHAPTER TWO

IRONMAN: RACE DAY MINUS EIGHT DAYS

I ride the hills to East Fork Lake and back, a distance of twenty-five miles, one last time on the Saturday before race week and then complete a short run after that, thinking about my final preparations for the race. On Sunday, I am scheduled to run for an hour and spend an hour on the bike. My last workout will be on Wednesday, when I will ride forty-five minutes on the bike, followed by a fifteen-minute run. I will do nothing else the rest of the week. At that point I will be finished with my preparation. Either I will be able to complete the race or I won't. Earlier in the year I picked up a book entitled *Be Iron Fit*, which is a training manual for people with busy schedules who want to complete an Ironman. Three different programs are offered: Just Make It, Intermediate, and Competitive. During the training year I have tried to get in as much of the Competitive Program as I could, and yet in my last week of preparation I am just hoping to finish the race.

My initial plan is to go down to Louisville on Saturday and register for the race. That changes when I read the Athlete's Manual, which states that athletes can register only on Thursday and Friday. Anyone who is not registered by 5:00 on Friday cannot race. Given these time restrictions, I decide to leave work before noon on Friday to allow myself plenty of time to get to Louisville before registration closes. My plan is to register for the race, walk around the exhibit hall, attend the dinner for the athletes and the mandatory meeting following the dinner, and finally drive back to Cincinnati and be in bed by 11:00.

I make it to Louisville around 2:30 p.m. and find the Galt Hotel, where the registration and exhibit hall are located. There are multiple stages to completing the registration. At the first table I have to show my driver's license. Then I have to go to another table to sign a waiver and release. The release states, in essence, if something happens to me during the race, it is my tough luck. They also ask for next of kin, which only plants seeds of doubt that I will actually live through the event. At the next table, I am handed a packet which contains my race number and assorted stickers to affix to my helmet, bike and transition bag. I look at my race number, which is 2927, and note that there are 3050 athletes registered for the race. I conclude this is their prediction of either my order of finish or the year I will finish the race. At the next table, I receive my racing chip, which will go around my left ankle on race day. Finally, at the last table I receive a backpack in which I will transport my gear to the race. The only exit from the registration area is through the merchandise area. (I think they plan it this way.) I pick up a water bottle to buy, but put it back when I see how long the lines are.

I exit the merchandise area and then walk through the exhibit hall. While dinner is several hours away, I am hungry now, so I keep dropping by the nutrition exhibits to stuff myself on their free samples. Across the hall is the bicycle store, so I go inside.

In training for a long event, I have learned that a long time in a bicycle saddle can cause blisters in the most unlikely and unmentionable spots. I notice a product called Butt'r, which is a lubricant for such occasions, and decide to spring for $3.00 and complete the purchase, making my major purchase of the day. I ask the cashier, "Do you squirt this directly into your biking shorts or do you apply it directly?"

"You apply it directly," he responds. I thank him and start to leave the store. Now that I have seen all the exhibits, I wonder how I will kill the next few hours until the banquet. Then I spot a man walking by, carrying a bicycle wheel. We exchange greetings and introductions. He is Kurt Miller from Austin, Texas, an engineer by profession who will be competing in the fifty-year-old division.

"Have you ever done an Ironman before?" I ask.

He replies, "I tried one last year, but I had to drop out because I became dehydrated." I file this information away for future reference. He then continues, "This year I hired a professional coach."

I think, "Wow, there are some really serious individuals in this race." (I learn later that he does finish the race this year.) We talk for some time and then agree to go to the banquet together, since neither of us will have family in town until the next day.

I decide to get off my feet, so I go sit in the lobby area. A younger man from Chattanooga sits across from me. I find out that this is his second year at the Louisville competition. I ask him about the bike course, and he says it is hilly. His parents soon join him, and we begin to talk. I see his father staring at me quizzically, and after looking me over he says, "Just how old are you?"

"I am 59," I answer.

His jaw drops and he says, "Why, that is my age!"

I reply, "I figure it is now or never for me."

I meet Kurt for dinner, and 3,000 athletes and their families and friends are also in attendance. The dinner is inspiring. We sit with a team from Toronto, Canada, that participates in a number of these events each year. It is invigorating to be with a group of healthy, positive people. After dinner they show a video of the event, including all the frenzy and activity of the swim, bike and run. I am pumped. The next video features an athlete who did not complete the race the previous year. She had to drop out at mile nine of the run due to exhaustion. "Are they trying to tell me something?" I wonder. This athlete is trying again this year to complete the race.

The race director next offers some statistics. All fifty states are represented as well as twenty-five countries. I look in the book they have given me, and there are only twenty-nine of these major Ironman events worldwide each year, six of which are held in the United States. The rest are all over the world. Louisville is by far the closest to me. In this year's race, seventy-five percent of the participants are men and the balance are women. The largest number of men is in the forty to forty-five age division, while for the women it is in thirty to thirty-five age division. I notice that while many of the athletes are like me, in that they just want to complete an Ironman, there are also many who have already completed several of these events, and they know how to race.

The race cut-off times are also announced. These are the times that participants must meet for each stage of the race in order to continue to the next stage. The times become increasingly difficult to meet as the race progresses. The swim cut-off is two hours and twenty minutes after the last swimmer enters the water. "This will be no problem," I think. The first lap of the bike segment needs to be completed by 2:30 in the afternoon, and the completion time for the bike is at 6:30 in the evening. The second lap of the run has to start by 9:25 p.m. and the race ends at midnight regardless of when you start. This time restriction will prove to be an important factor for me.

The banquet ends, and I wish Kurt well in the race as I leave to drive home. I make it home in time to be in bed by 11:00 as planned. In a little under 49 hours, I will need to be crossing the finish line. I feel my energy focusing on that big day as I try to sleep.

HANG WITH POSITIVE PEOPLE

CHAPTER THREE

IRONMAN: RACE DAY MINUS ONE DAY

I am up early the next morning to complete my packing. My wife, Gretchen, and I head to the event, meeting Gretchen's sister, Barb, and Stu at the hotel.

I have to check my bike in by 5:00, which is our first priority. We get to the bike transition area and Stu nudges me. He knows his bikes. "Do you see some of those bikes?" he whispers. I nod. "Why, some of those tri-bikes cost between $5,000 and $7,000. There is some serious money in the equipment here." I again nod in agreement. The tri-bikes are designed for the triathlon. The rider hunches over in a time-trial position for the duration of the race. These bikes are not only designed to reduce wind resistance, but they also require the use of different leg muscles, which makes the run easier. My bike is a good road bike. I bought it nine years ago as a present to myself when I turned fifty. It has a metal frame and is heavier than the newer bikes, which are built from ultra-light composite materials. I consider it more than adequate to get the job done, especially since I do not think I can last eight hours hunched over my handlebars. Sitting in an upright position will be more comfortable for me. Also, during the past several years I have had other spending priorities, such as my children's college education, a wedding, braces, and just basic living expenses, which would not have justified that type of investment.

We complete the bike registration, and I leave my bike in the transition area for the race. Stu and I want to drive as much of the course as we can before dinner to get a feel for how difficult it is. I have heard so many people say it is tough that the fears have grown in my mind. As we drive, I notice that the first ten miles are flat, as everyone has said. During the next ten miles, the hills begin. The first major hill is at mile eleven, which is a one-mile uphill climb. I examine the incline and think, "At least from the car this hill is not as steep as some of the hills I ride at East Fork." I begin to feel relieved and slightly more confident.

We look at the hills on the out-and-back on KY-1964, and I come to the same conclusion. I have trained on some major hills and feel the course is difficult but not impossible. We continue to the town of La Grange, where I hope my family will watch me pass through the next day.

Since it is now getting late, we drive back to Louisville and try to find a restaurant, which proves to be one of the greatest challenges of the day. The downtown restaurants are understandably packed, so we can only find space at an Italian restaurant on the outer edges of the loop around town. After dinner, I plan to go to bed early. Stu is going to accompany me to the start of the swim segment in the morning. We begin to work backwards to calculate when we should leave. I want to be in line for the swim an hour early, which according to my calculations would place me in mid-position for the start of the swim. "Who in their right mind would get there earlier than that?" I reason. What I did not calculate correctly is that these are aspiring Ironman athletes and they are not in their right minds! No one in their right mind would pay an entry fee of $600 to do this to their body. I should have known better, and it was nearly a fatal error the next day. Oh, silly me.

Stu and I agree to meet outside my door at 5:20 a.m., which will allow enough time to drop off water bottles for the bike portion of the race and then walk to the swim area. I set my alarm for 4:50 a.m. While getting ready for bed I reach for my toothbrush in my overnight bag and instead find the edge of my razor blade, cutting my finger. It starts to bleed a lot. I am amazed at how much blood a cut on the finger can produce. After soaking through several tissues the bleeding finally stops, and Gretchen gives me a bandage to put over the cut. I then try to go to sleep. I finally fall asleep but waken after a short time. Pre-race jitters and fears are preventing me from sleeping. I go to the bathroom a number of times. Boisterous party-goers interrupt my rest again at 2:30 a.m. and police sirens blare continually throughout the night. I only manage to get several hours of sleep and am exhausted by the time I have to get up. At this point, I am worried. There is nothing like trying to do an Ironman after pulling a virtual all-nighter.

While I am exhausted from lack of sleep, I am pleased that my family and Stu are there to support me and cheer me on during the race. Stu has always been the brother I never had, so his encouraging presence will mean so much during the race.

STU'S JOURNEY

Just as I needed encouragement during my race, Stu needed total support for his recovery. With his energy drained, no appetite, sores in his mouth, tubes sticking in all openings in his body, and his body wracked with fever, Stu could barely continue.

At this point, his wife provided the support and encouragement he needed. Barb told Stu he had to have a positive attitude and keep going. She became an inspiration to Stu and his nurses. On one of those tough days, Stu's mom gave him a letter telling him to get a grip and look forward to the future. Stu envisioned eating Thanksgiving dinner with his family. Although this was nine months away, it became a goal for him to shoot for.

But then he got graft-vs.-host disease. The bone marrow Steve had donated to Stu began to attack Stu's body. Stu was given a flurry of drugs to suppress it. Stu's doctor was tough. He said that he did not care how high a fever Stu had; he expected Stu to get out of bed and start using his stationary bike. Across the hall from Stu's hospital room was a man in his early twenties who had also had a transplant. The nurses told Stu that this man rode twenty minutes a day on the bike, and they challenged Stu to do the same. Stu started riding his bike.

After forty-two days in the hospital, Stu was very eager to leave. His friend across the hall was scheduled to leave on Saturday, and Stu wanted to leave at the same time. When Saturday came, Stu asked if his friend had left and was told that he had a setback. Stu was discharged. When he asked about his friend two weeks later, he learned that his friend had died. When Stu asked himself why he was spared and his friend was not, he realized that his positive attitude had helped. Of the four people who had a transplant at the same time, Stu was the only one to survive. The lesson of positive encouragement became embedded in the core of Stu's being.

FURTHER REFLECTION

Everyone needs encouragement, but words can also wound. Sometimes words can wound so deeply that the wounds stay with you all your life. I remember when I was in grade school, one of my friends called me a cretin. When he called me this, I did not know what a cretin was, but it sure did not sound good. I looked up the word and learned that a cretin is defined as a deformed idiot. I do not know if he was trying out a new vocabulary word or if there were an element of truth in his statement, but in any event a wound was opened. Of all the experiences I have had in life, many of which have been forgotten, this is something I still remember.

Alternatively, it is amazing what the power of positive words can do. I had some friends who owned a diner in downtown Cincinnati. One of their customers was a man they called Smokey. He got this name, not because he smoked, but because he was poor, and the only item he could afford was a cup of coffee. He would loiter over the coffee and slowly add cream to his cup and then stir while watching the cream turn the black coffee into a light shade of brown. He was looking for a job but could not find one. This went on for many months. My friends would offer words of encouragement to him, and I think this was one of the reasons he kept returning to their restaurant. One day Smokey came in all smiles. He told my friends that he had found a job. My friends were delighted with the news. Their restaurant was not large, and many of the customers were regulars who knew Smokey. One of my friends tapped on a glass and asked for everyone's attention. He got on a chair and said, "I have an announcement to make. Smokey got a job." Everyone applauded.

Another example of the power of positive words is this story, which I remember hearing around a college fraternity lunch table: One of my fraternity brothers, Gordon, coached a youth basketball team. The team he coached was just learning to play the game, and the scores of the games were never high. In fact, the basketballs were about as big as the kids. During one game, his team was down by thirteen points at half time, which was an incredible obstacle to overcome given the age of his players. One of his players asked, "Coach, do you think we can win?" Gordon responded, "Look, the other team scored all those points in the first half. There is no reason you cannot do the same in the second half." As he was telling the story my friend said, "You know, I scarcely believed a word I told them, because their deficit was so large at half time. But you know what? They believed me, and sure enough, they played terrific defense in the second half and scored more points than the other team did in the first half and came back and won."

Sometimes, just being near positive people is enough; they don't even have to use words. I remember one such time when one of my businesses experienced a huge economic reversal. It was devastating, and I found that in my mid-fifties I needed to pick up the pieces and begin anew. I was extremely depressed and felt abandoned and alone. A friend of mine who is a pastor called me, and we had lunch. I poured out my heart to him and peppered him with questions as he listened to me bare my soul. I cannot remember the advice he gave, but he was just there to listen and not condemn.

My mother died of cancer at the young age of 64. As I was leaving the hospital after she died, I bumped into an acquaintance on the way out. He asked who I was visiting and I told him, "My mother has just died." He did not know what to say other than that he was sorry. He was a friend but not a close friend; however, he showed up for her funeral. His presence meant more to me than words could ever convey.

As usual, Stu taught me a lesson in staying positive. In

college, I minored in economics, which is often called "the dismal science," because as a field of study, it deals with the allocation of scarce resources. Since that time I have enjoyed reading books about economics and politics. One recent book was entitled *China, Inc.*, which deals with how the Chinese economic juggernaut is taking over the world. I was visibly distressed by this message, but Stu chided me, saying, "There is no reason to be so upset by what you are reading. There are some things you cannot control and you shouldn't worry about them. Just focus on those things you can control. I periodically take a 'news fast' so I do not become overwhelmed by what is happening in the world."

Preparing to compete in the Ironman was such a daunting task for me that I needed all the support and encouragement I could get. One of my particular enjoyments is Masters Swimming. Two days a week I get up at 4:50 in the morning in order to be in the pool by 5:30. The workouts are intense. We swim hard for one hour and fifteen minutes, and I am exhausted yet invigorated when I finish with practice. While the workouts get the heart rate rising and blood flowing, the best part of it are the people. Everyone is so encouraging and supportive. These are all competitive athletes who are striving to do their best. A number of them have completed an Ironman, many were stars in college, and some use this for cross-training. All, however, are supportive and push me to do my best.

One of my favorite Masters Swimming companions is my friend Perry, who is my age and places at the top of his age group in triathlons. When we are assigned a particularly difficult set of repeats, he says simply, "You can do this." And, you know, we do. You need to hang with people like this. Life is hard, and it can beat you down. Hang with people who are uplifting and supportive. Then you will be able to support others in the same way.

LIVE BEYOND YOURSELF

CHAPTER FOUR

IRONMAN: RACE DAY AUGUST 26, 2012

The alarm does not need to go off. I am already awake. I shave this time without cutting myself, get dressed and meet Stu at our appointed time. I eat three energy bars and have two nutritional drinks as my breakfast before the race. We walk to the bike transition area, where I drop off my water bottles and put power bars into my transition bag. We then begin walking to the start of the swim, which is a mile away. When we get closer, a race volunteer marks my race number on my leg and arm using a permanent marker. I am so beside myself with nerves and lack of sleep that I begin to gag, and Stu gives me a look of grave concern. I know that he is thinking, "How can he get sick before the race even begins?"

We become aware that the line has already formed for the swim, and it extends as far as the eye can see. We keep walking and walking. Still there is no end to the line. We walk for over a mile before we finally reach the end. I then realize that most of these people have been in line since

5:00, which means that they had to get up around 4:00 a.m. I later learn that there is a limit to how early participants can show up before the race; otherwise, people would wait through the night to be first in line.

I look at my place and realize I am near the end of the line. Rather than getting in the water by 7:15 as I had planned, I will be one of the last swimmers entering the water and will still need to complete the race by midnight. From this point on, everything will be focused on making it before that critical midnight deadline. I think, "What a costly and fatal miscalculation this could prove to be!" I am annoyed at myself, but there is nothing I can do at this point.

To someone who is not comfortable swimming in the open water, the swim portion can be an exercise in unbridled terror. As opposed to the clear water, lane lines, and being able to touch the bottom of a pool, an open water swim in the Ohio River is completely different. Visibility is only several feet, and you have no idea how deep the water is. It is a free-for-all as swimmers vie for position, meaning there is a possibility of getting kicked in the face or nose or of having someone rip off your swim goggles as they swim past. The race has the frenzy of a school of fish being chased by a great white shark which is rapidly gaining ground. It is like swimming in a blender. As if this weren't enough, you have drifting logs, waves from barge traffic and the mental image of the giant prehistoric-looking spoonbill catfish (which can grow as big as a man) lurking below the surface, ready to take a bite out of your leg. Tempting you are the officials in kayaks. If you get kicked in the face and have to stop and happen to grab the side of the kayak to save your life, you are disqualified if the kayak makes any forward progress. The choice is yours: save your life and be disqualified, or shake it off and continue the race.

The wait is now over. I hear a cannon go off in the distance, announcing the start of the pro division. Several minutes later I hear another cannon go off, and the event begins. The line inches forward. As we get closer to the start, the line moves faster. I can finally see the start of the race, where they are lining up swimmers who are jumping into the water six at a time. I hear someone call my name. It is my friend Jeremy from Masters Swimming, who is helping as a race official. He wishes me well as I line up with six others and jump into the water. My giant journey has begun.

STU'S JOURNEY

As I begin my swim, I know I am in for a long day. But my one long day is nothing compared to Stu's long road to recovery. It was six months after the transplant before Stu was able to go back to work. After one year, he began to feel better. After Stu returned to full-time work, his secretary showed him an article about how the actor Paul Newman was starting a camp in Connecticut for kids with cancer. Newman's goal was to help children who had gone through what Stu had experienced. He purchased property for the camp and sponsored the children's expenses for two-week sessions. Anyone with leukemia, cancer, or a blood-related disease was invited. Stu wrote and asked if he could be a counselor. The timing was perfect. The camp accepted both Stu and Barb as volunteers. Stu ended up counseling there three years in a row.

The first year, Stu took a two-week vacation from work, and with Barb, drove to Connecticut from Chicago. During the drive, he noticed a burning sensation on his skin. At the camp the first morning, Stu got up and still felt the burning. He went to the camp doctor, who immediately placed him in quarantine. Stu had developed a case of the shingles, which is caused by the chicken pox virus and is very contagious. If he had not been diagnosed quickly, he could have exposed many campers to this virus, which would have been extremely dangerous for children who were immunosuppressed.

Stu was sent to Yale University Hospital and ended up staying in the hospital for eleven days. He was released just in time to join Barb for the closing ceremony at camp, after which they drove two days back to Chicago, and Stu returned to work. So much for summer vacation! After hearing Barb's camp stories, however, Stu vowed to go back.

They returned the next year, and this time Stu was able to stay for the complete session. He said he got more out of the camp than he was able to give. Especially meaningful were the evening cabin chats, where children, including some from the inner-city New York, opened up and drew strength from each other.

There was one young boy from New York City who was tough and hard, or so it appeared. He put on a veneer of toughness as a defense. However, once this veneer was penetrated, beneath the surface was a scared little boy who was grappling with his life- threatening illness. He always wore a bandana to cover his head, which was bald from his cancer treatment. One day when he went swimming, his bandana fell off when he dove in, and he began to panic. Stu, who was in the water at the time, saw what was happening and swam over to meet him. He retrieved the bandana, and said, "Do you think people care that your bandana fell off? Look at all these other kids. They do not have hair, either. Just relax and enjoy yourself." After this talk with Stu, the boy relaxed and began to enjoy his time in the water.

Another time, Stu was getting dressed, and a camper pointed to the port-a-cath in Stu's chest, which was used to administer cancer treatment, and said, "So you have one of those, too?" Nothing more needed to be said. The camper realized that he was not alone, but that Stu and others were going through the same thing he was. This story illustrates the concept of the *wounded healer*. Those who have gone through a similar experience are best able to understand and help others. We often wonder why we have to suffer. Perhaps the purpose in all this is to enable us to help others who are going through the same walk.

Stu appreciates life more now for having gone through his experience with cancer. He doesn't get too comfortable with life. He will not put his job before his family. Now he has a sense that there are more important things in life than work. He makes sure he spends time with his family doing things of value.

FURTHER REFLECTION

Training for the Ironman was a joy, because in dedicating the race to Stu I felt his story could be told and people could draw inspiration from that. By living outside of myself and looking beyond my immediate problems, I realize how fortunate I am.

I have learned from experience that those times when I have given of myself unselfishly and have not expected anything in return, I have gained far more than I have given. Sometimes this is in the form of a monetary gain. Once, I volunteered to help in a United Way Campaign. During the course of helping my local community in this way, I had the opportunity to meet an Executive Vice President of a local bank. We became friends through our work on this project, and this bank became our largest customer.

Not every benefit is monetary. Sometimes the reward is just glowing in the satisfaction of helping someone. When I was around five years old, I remember my mother taking my sister and me to a local supermarket. In addition to food, this store had a toy section. My sister spotted some plastic dinosaurs, and it was obvious she wanted one. I took some of the few dollars in my pockets and bought her these plastic toys. I bought them because she was my sister, and I wanted to do something for her. There was no other reason. I remember how good I felt with this simple act. I remember skipping in the parking lot. I have forgotten many of my life experiences, but this is one I remember after all these years.

I remember a proverb that says if we water others, we will be watered. That is true. When we give of ourselves, we are blessed.

GO BIG OR GO HOME

CHAPTER FIVE

**IRONMAN: SIXTEEN HOURS TWENTY MINUTES
UNTIL MIDNIGHT**

After I hit the water, I feel better. Now I am doing something, instead of just being eaten up by my nerves. My plan is to use the first five minutes of swimming as a warm-up and then gradually increase my pace. The water is crowded with swimmers. The initial 800 meters involves swimming upstream around an island. This island is on my left and I breathe on my left, so it is easy to keep my distance and not get hung up on a log or debris. I continue past the island, swimming upstream towards a yellow buoy for another 500 meters or so. I reach the buoy, swim around it, and begin to follow a line of buoys and swimmers into the distance. I track my progress by the buoys I pass and the bridges I swim under. I feel good on the swim and notice I am passing a lot of swimmers. This bolsters my confidence. When I come upon a group of swimmers clustered together, I do breaststroke until I can plot a path through their midst. This takes some time, and occasionally my pathway is circuitous. I am now in the midst of the biggest athletic endeavor I have ever attempted.

STU'S JOURNEY

Sometimes going big involves initial small steps. As Stu continued to get back in shape, he decided to run a 5k race. He had worked himself up from running one mile to three miles and felt ready to compete in the 5k. After completing this, he met a man named Jim Frontier who suggested that he should try running a triathlon. Stu had always been intrigued by the triathlon, so he decided to go for it. He trained hard all summer. As he got back into decent shape, he began to feel better and better. As Stu's condition improved, Stu and his brother Steve challenged each other to run the Lake Geneva triathlon. This event was challenging in itself, but even more so now, considering that Stu was recovering from cancer. The course consisted of a mile swim in Lake Geneva, a fifteen-mile bike ride, and a 10,000-meter run. Stu and Steve created their own fundraiser for Loyola University Hospital, which was to be used strictly for research. They raised almost $11,000 just by word of mouth.

I told Stu I wanted to run the Chicago Marathon. Stu thought this was great and declared he would run the last ten miles with me. He met me at the sixteen-mile mark and provided the encouragement that helped me finish the race. The electric atmosphere of that event inspired Stu to try running a marathon himself.

Stu investigated several training programs until he found one that was perfect. The Leukemia Society had a program called "Team in Training," which custom-designs a program for its participants. It is the runner's job to raise money for the program, which goes to families of leukemia patients to help them with expenses such as driving to the treatment. Stu was the second largest fundraiser in the Chicago area.

After a year of training, Stu was ready for the Chicago Marathon. I also put in considerable training and hoped to improve my time from the previous year. We arrived in Chicago by mid-afternoon the day before the big race. Advertisements said that over thirteen thousand runners were expected to participate in the Chicago Marathon. When we arrived at Stu's home, he greeted me with a severe cough that wracked his whole body. I could tell he was nervous about attempting to run a complete marathon when he was not feeling well, but it was not Stu's style to quit anything. That evening, we rented the movie *Chariots of Fire* to give us inspiration for the next day. We also ate a light pasta dinner, which provided necessary carbohydrates for the race and was easy on the stomach. Stu still had a deep and wrenching cough.

Because of his cough, Stu had trouble sleeping. So as not to disturb his wife, he pulled the covers over his head, took out a flashlight, and started to read an article by Frank Shorter, the first American to win an Olympic marathon, which happened in the 1972 Olympics in Munich, Germany. The article said that although training was important and proper diet was important, the most important aspect of achieving a strong marathon performance was a good night's rest. Stu coughed some more as he contemplated these words.

I was awakened at 5:10 by a knock on my door. I quickly got dressed and pulled on my sweats. It was cold outside, around thirty-eight degrees. We found a place to park several blocks away from the starting line and stopped by a hotel to make one last pit stop before the race. At this point the butterflies began. We hustled to the starting line, found the marker where those who hoped to hold a pace of nine minutes per mile would start, and got ready for the starting gun.

People were packed into the starting gate, all thirteen thousand of them. There were helicopters hovering overhead, taking pictures of the race's start. The runners were in a festive mood. A countdown began, and the gun went off.

Several miles into the race, we picked up the pace as the runners thinned out. Our plan was to try to hold a pace of nine minutes per mile, but Stu and Jim were running under this pace. We started out at a pace of 8:50 minutes per mile and gradually picked up the pace to 8:40 minutes per mile. I saw Stu staring straight ahead and knew he was totally focused. He did not look to the right or left but kept his gaze on the road and his mind on the task before him.

The course for the marathon winds its way through the various sections of the city. Everywhere we went, people were cheering and providing words of encouragement. In the projects, several girls gave us high-fives as we passed. In the Mexican neighborhood, there was a band playing. Chinatown had a dragon weaving its way through the runners. The entire mood was festive, and each section provided some interesting distractions.

As we passed the halfway point, I looked up at the clock and read that we had completed half the race in less than two hours at 1:57. While we were ahead of our intended pace, because it had even taken several minutes just to get to the starting line, I felt that I could not sustain our current pace for the balance of the race. At the fifteen-mile mark I started getting sick, and by the eighteen-mile mark I was really hurting. Stu and Jim were long gone. The crowds were gone. It was a lonely stretch of road, and by this time, my mind was telling me to quit. I stopped running and tried to collect my thoughts. I began walking and tried to catch my breath. After several minutes of walking, I willed myself to continue. That couple of minutes of walking allowed me enough rest to continue.

There is a lesson in this: God does allow us to rest. When fatigue hits in the course of life, we should rest in God, then continue on. The last four miles of the race were a straight shot down the lakeshore. I had to concentrate to keep my feet moving. I crossed the finish line feeling faint from dehydration. I had improved my time over the previous years by about a minute and a half. Stu and Jim had finished about eight minutes ahead of me. Later I told Gretchen, "If I ever get the urge to run another marathon, please talk me out of it."

After that race, Stu concentrated on biking and triathlons. Stu is a good athlete, and he was able to complete an Olympic-distance triathlon in under three hours. In fact, while in high school Stu set the school record for the mile run, which I believe still stands. One day I was running a set of 440s at the track. I ran the last one as hard as I could, and Stu watched and decided to run one, too. I watched him and could not but be impressed by the grace and smoothness of his stride. He ran with the fluid motion of a gazelle.

FURTHER REFLECTION

When I decided to sign up for the Ironman, I began searching the Internet to find training advice. I came across one website where a man had written, "Go big or go home." This caught my eye. Sometimes you just have to go for a goal which is so large that you do not know whether you will succeed. The Ironman was just such a goal. I had run several marathons, but had never trained for something of this magnitude. The idea of training for and completing an Ironman was daunting, for it was an incredibly large goal.

My first attempt at going big was more than forty years ago. When I was in high school, I desperately wanted to be a starter on my high school basketball team. I played well my sophomore year and ended the season with seventeen points in the final game. I thought I had a good chance of starting on the varsity squad by the time I was a senior. Life has a way of adding twists and turns. During the summer, our coach resigned, and he was replaced by a coach who believed in a slower, more deliberate style of offense. Despite all the hours of practice, all I could do was ride the bench my junior year. I was simply not good enough to make the starting five that year. In my senior year, I was vying for a starting spot with a gifted junior. We had won our first four games, and he got the nod to go against our rivals, who were also undefeated. In that game, our coach did not make one substitution during the entire game. We won, and the headlines read, "Mariemont's Iron Five Defeat Milford." That game spelled the end of my goal. If you watch a team during a game, the players on the bench lean forward as they intently watch the game. To try to get in the game, I would lean back to catch the coach's eye, hoping he would put me in. He would look at me, roll his eyes and put in someone else. This experience caused me considerable frustration.

To vent my frustrations, I would daydream. There was a book in our library about the Olympic Games. I would read this book for hours and daydream about something greater. Perhaps there was some sport that I could actually be good in. "Surely there must be some sport on this planet in which I could excel," I reasoned. While reading this book I came across a sport called the Modern Pentathlon. It combines five sports consisting of the five skills a field courier might have needed during the days of Napoleon. The general would give the field courier an important message, and the courier would mount his horse and race across the countryside to deliver the message. He would have to jump fences, cross streams and negotiate other obstacles. He was in enemy territory, and perhaps his horse would be shot out from under him. He would then take out his pistol and dispose of several enemy soldiers. When he ran out of bullets, he might have taken his sword and dueled with more enemies. The enemy might still be pursuing him, and he would have to swim across a river to escape. He would then run the rest of the way to deliver the message.

I thought, "This is the sport for me! While I may not be the best at an individual sport, perhaps I could be good enough in five sports to excel in this event. I had never participated in any of these sports, and I did not know where to begin. I called the United States Olympic Committee to ask their advice, and they sent me a nice packet of information in the mail. At that time, the United States Modern Pentathlon team trained at Fort Sam Houston, Texas, which is an army base. (Now the team trains in Colorado Springs.) This packet of information contained the cut-off times needed to qualify to train at the center. The information also stated if you were not already a good swimmer, it was too late. I had never swum competitively before, so I resolved to concentrate on swimming.

Basketball season was winding up. There was a swim team that practiced right after basketball practice, so I donned my swimsuit and asked the coach if I could practice with them. My basketball coach found out what I had done, and I was politely told not to practice with the swim team until after basketball season ended. I decided to defer any future swimming until college.

I was accepted into Vanderbilt University, and shortly after I began my freshman year, I checked with the swim coach, John Smith, who at one time held the world record in the backstroke. He smiled and agreed to let me train with the team, informing me that team practice was about to begin.

The following week I showed up for my first team practice. There were the varsity swimmers and about fifteen freshmen. When I walked onto the swim deck getting ready for practice, I was surrounded by several of the varsity swimmers. The team captain, John Stein, was a tall sprinter with a narrow waist and massive shoulders. He gazed at me, studying the specimen before him. At that time I weighed only 135 pounds and did not have much muscle mass. "What do you swim?" he asked, trying to figure out what event I could possibly do. I had no clue as to the distances or events. All I knew was that the pentathlon swim was freestyle, so I scanned the record board which was mounted behind his shoulder and searched for an event. The pentathlon swim was 300 meters and I found a distance close to that event and I blurted out, "I swim the 200 free."

He followed with a question, "What are your times?"

"I don't have a time," I stated simply. I saw a look of total puzzlement and stunned silence as he tried to process this information. I could almost read his thoughts: "What do you mean that you do not have a time?"

"What?" was all he could muster.

"I have never been on a swim team before, and I do not have a time for an event. I would like to try out for the team," I offered.

They shook their heads in wonderment as the coach then strode out of the office and directed the team to get into the water. I did not realize what I was up against. Most of the swimmers on this team had won their state championships in high school and were competitive at the college level.

I remember that after the first workout, my arms were so sore I could barely pull on my pants. I was so slow that when the other swimmers would get ready to pass me, I would dive to the bottom of the pool, wait for them to pass, and then continue swimming. The number of freshmen on the team quickly dwindled down to around six, as people realized it was too hard to both swim and study. I hung in there and gradually improved.

After several months of swimming, I asked the coach to time me in a 325-yard swim, which was close to the 300 meters I was training for. I mounted the starting blocks, and on the whistle, I swam as hard as I could for the entire distance. Around 200 yards into the swim, my arms felt like lead, my lungs were on fire and my legs were numb. I plowed ahead to the finish. I was exhausted. "Surely I have just broken an Olympic record by my effort," I thought. The coach announced my time, and I realized I was about a minute off from the time I believed was necessary to qualify for a clinic at Fort Sam Houston. In swimming that is an eternity. I lay on the deck of the pool, as I contemplated just how high the mountain was that I would have to climb.

I hung in there for the rest of the year, and my times gradually improved. I also joined the fencing club, which allowed me to take up another sport that was part of the pentathlon. This was a wonderful experience, because we got to travel around the country and compete against other collegiate teams. I improved in that as well, and that became my best sport in the pentathlon.

After my sophomore year, my times had improved enough that I decided to apply for a clinic. I was delighted when I was accepted. I was off to San Antonio for a month-long clinic. There were around ten participants in the clinic, and most were younger than I. However, one athlete, Shawn Hasson, was my age. He was a swimmer from California who looked like someone out of a surfing magazine. We quickly became friends.

Because San Antonio is in southern Texas, our training day needed to start early before the oppressive heat of the day set in. We were awakened shortly after 5:00 every morning. For a college student who was used to staying up late and sleeping longer, such an early start was tough. However, I did develop an appreciation for early-morning workouts. There is nothing like beginning a workout before the sun rises and watching the sun come up on a new day. We did our swim workouts at the fifty-meter pool at the Lone Star Brewery. In addition to producing beer, they also made root beer which they would give us after a workout. I always looked forward to that.

Fencing was taught by a massive Swede by the name of Kye. He was in excess of 6'3" in height, and for the training sessions he would wear a large protective leather vest. When he stood on the fencing strip I felt like I was facing Goliath. He would speak to us in broken English, which I had trouble understanding. "Z point before z foot," he would bark as he commanded us to begin our attack. I wondered, "What on earth is a z point?" When we did not perform the attack to his satisfaction, he would whip his blade and smack us on the rear as we went by. There is nothing like the feel of cold steel to get your attention. After a while, I figured out that what he was trying to say was, "The point before the foot," which meant that he wanted the point of the blade to hit his body before the foot hit the mat from the lunge.

Pistol shooting was taught by Harry, who ironically had fought for the Germans during World War II. He was a great coach, who taught us how to align the sights and control our breathing as we were shooting. Once he showed me that I did not even need to see the target to hit it. He had me align my sights and remain still. He then held a piece of paper in front of my pistol and had me squeeze the trigger. I did, and the shot went through the paper and hit the target.

We got to train with some of the athletes who were aspiring to represent the United States in the Olympics and the World Championships. Their ability was amazing. Some could run close to four minutes in the mile and swim 300 meters in a little over three minutes. Both of these times are very fast. I could not help but look at them with wonder and amazement.

At the end of the clinic there was a competition. However, my friend Shawn had broken his foot while running around the parade field. He had stepped into a hole and suffered a stress fracture. That paved the way for me to do well. I had a good competition and won our clinic. I was invited back the next year to compete in the junior division.

The competition the following year was a quantum leap tougher than the prior year. I was competing with athletes who were closer to me in age. I did not do as well at the junior level. My best time in the mile was 5:17, and in the swim it was around 3:40. Participants are awarded a certain number of points for every second in the run and swim, and even if I had been able to match the performance of the others in the skill sports of fencing, riding and pistol shooting, such achievement would be not have been enough to offset their athletic advantage in swimming and running. My finish in the junior division was disappointing, and I decided to see how much I could improve in swimming in my senior year before deciding whether to continue pursuing this dream.

Of the freshmen who started with me, there was just one other who remained on the team our senior year. While I trained hard, my times barely improved. When I realized that I had plateaued in swimming, I had to face reality. My heart urged me to continue, but my head told me differently. I knew that based on my times in the swim and run I was not competitive with the more gifted athletes, and the simple reality was that my chances of making any national team were remote at best. I had given it my best, so I decided instead to enroll in law school in the fall.

As I reflect back on this particular journey, I did not realize it at the time but this experience provided the foundation to allow me to attempt an Ironman competition forty years later. I had learned to swim, and had I not tried out for the college swim team I doubt I would have tried swimming many years later. I also took up fencing again after completing law school and managed to qualify for and compete in three U.S. National Championships. Finally, I also developed a love for early morning workouts. I run before work, and then my workout is done for the day. Also, it mellows me out, so I am better able to deal with the pressures of work later. Yes, if you go big, you never know where it will lead.

EMBRACE LIFE'S DETOURS

CHAPTER SIX

IRONMAN: SIXTEEN HOURS UNTIL MIDNIGHT

I do not know how many extra yards I swim while trying to get around all those swimmers. I know it is a lot. Also, since there are no lane lines, it is hard to swim in a straight line. The best I can do is to focus on the next buoy and head toward that.

STU'S JOURNEY

Sometimes life does not always lead us on a straight path toward our destination, and there are detours along the way. Certainly Stu has had his share of detours in his life's journey.

My relationship with Stu is much like that of the Harlem Globetrotters and the Washington Generals, which is the team the Globetrotters play against. Try as I might, I rarely beat Stu in anything. I looked up the record of the Washington Generals against the Globetrotters, and it is 6 wins and 13,000 losses. Yes, that is a good analogy.

I can just imagine what the Generals' locker room is like when they win. I am sure it is pandemonium. It must be like a baseball team from Iceland beating the New York Yankees in the World Series.

Since I am competitive by nature, it is frustrating that no matter how hard I try I cannot beat Stu. However, one day in particular is etched in my memory. Stu was down for a visit, and we rode our bikes to East Fork Lake. The course is hilly, and on the way back there is one hill that is incredibly steep. That day I was stronger than Stu on that hill and I waited for him at the top. I was elated and felt like dancing on my handle bars. "I have finally beaten Stu at something," I thought. I could tell something was wrong, however, because Stu was out of breath, which is not like him. Stu just shrugged it off saying that he felt a little tired.

Several weeks later he went in for tests and discovered that he had severe hepatitis in his liver. His liver was in severe distress. I realized it had only been possible for me to beat Stu when he had about three red blood cells traveling through his system providing oxygen. Stu had contracted hepatitis during all those blood transfusions following his chemotherapy and bone marrow transplant. Stu's liver was dying and so was he, unless a donor could be found.

Stu's name was added to the list for a liver transplant, and it became a waiting game. While playing golf one day, he received the call that a liver had been donated. Someone else's death became a gift of life for Stu. He was told to report to the hospital immediately, because there was limited time to perform the surgery. Fortunately, the surgery was successful, and another long road to recovery began. Stu concentrated on getting back into condition. Since his recovery from the liver transplant, he has completed several grueling century bike rides, the latest of which was through the mountains of Lake Tahoe. While having to undergo yet another surgery and transplant was certainly a detour in his recovery, Stu embraced and overcame his latest challenge. Now he is biking stronger than ever. And I still cannot beat him.

Even after his recovery, Stu has had his share of detours. He trained hard for a hundred mile ride in Tucson, Arizona. He and Barb flew down for the race. Stu got ready and was pedaling slowly toward the start. As he crossed some railroad tracks, his wheel slipped, and he crashed hard and landed on his head. He got back on his bike, but he does not even remember how he got to the start. He was asking questions that made no sense, and his companions realized that he had suffered a concussion. At that point his race was over.

This detour has not deterred him from continuing to ride, despite other medical issues. Stu's hips are shot and need to be replaced. All his treatments have destroyed the bone in the ball of his hip, so he is in pain from any activity. Still he soldiers on.

Stu has a cottage on Lake Michigan, and we often spend our vacation visiting him. Of course we have to do many bike rides. On our last visit I went for a ride with Stu and my son-in-law, Nate. We began our ride, and of course Stu was leading. The leader has the most difficult task, which is breaking the wind. The riders behind the leader have an easier time of it, because they are not fighting the wind. We rode faster and faster. My normal pace is around sixteen miles per hour, but we were now pushing twenty miles an hour. All I could do was tuck in behind Stu and Nate and desperately hang on, trying to keep up. The day was hot and windy, and yet Stu continued to lead. The wind was now in our faces, and we were traveling up a steep hill. I saw Stu reach into his back pocket and pull out something. He mercifully slowed down to eighteen miles per hour, and I was grateful for the break in pace. I then realized he was talking on his cell phone. "This is unbelievable," I thought. "Here is Stu riding uphill with hips so damaged that he needs to have them replaced, fighting headwinds that could flip a sailboat, talking on his cell phone and still maintaining a pace in excess of eighteen miles per hour. This is simply amazing!" I know that all the detours in his life have only made Stu stronger. I have the tired muscles to prove it.

FURTHER REFLECTION

One Saturday, I was scheduled to do a long bike ride. I had planned to attempt a full Ironman distance of 112 miles. This ride was designed to give me confidence that I could complete the distance on race day. However, I became concerned when I saw the weather forecast. The outlook was for oppressive heat of 105 degrees. On Friday evening we had a severe thunderstorm with high winds. I faced a choice for my ride the next day. I could take the Loveland Bike Trail which had a great deal of shade and would make my ride more comfortable. I recognized, however, that due to the wind storm the night before, the bike trail could be covered with a lot of debris. The other option was to do my usual route of East Fork Lake, which contained little shade, and I knew I would bake in the sun and heat.

I opted for the Loveland Bike Trail. I began my ride, and quickly found out that I had made the wrong choice. I had to dodge sticks and debris every several feet. Many branches had fallen on the trail. I had to travel slowly and pick my way through the branches. I hoped that the debris would let up, but it didn't. I approached Loveland, which was a distance of fourteen miles into my ride, only to discover that a large tree had fallen across the trail, blocking further progress. Several other cyclists were studying the tree, and they decided to abandon their ride and turn around. I followed them, thinking that my workout would surely be cut short.

When I approached Camp Dennison, I decided to do some of the hills in Indian Hill. I turned up Cunningham Road, which was a steeper hill than I had anticipated. It was so steep that I contemplated dismounting my bike and walking up the hill, but I imagined myself trying to unclip, falling in the road and being run over by a car, so I stayed on my bike and kept going. By the time I reached the top,

I was gulping air, trying to recover. After I had pedaled for several minutes, another cyclist came up behind me. I had not expected this. We began to talk and ride together. He knew the area well, and we both were having to adapt to a new workout routine. He suggested we do another hill. We rode downhill for a long time and then turned around and rode back up this same hill. My legs were still suffering from the Cunningham hill. He then suggested another hill, which we did. He was a much stronger biker than I am, and he would stop at the top of each hill and wait. I was grateful for his courtesy.

We went into Loveland, which was down a long hill. He said we should avoid the bike trail, and we could then retrace our route. Yes, there was another steep hill to climb outside of Loveland. In all that day we climbed 2000 feet in 56 miles, which is the same amount of climbing I would do on race day over the 112 miles. While I did not cover the distance I wanted, I sure got in plenty of hills. I had a challenging workout and had the fortune of making a new friend along the way. On Stu's road back to wholeness and health as well as on my quest to train for the Ironman, the lesson that we both needed to learn was to accept and embrace the detours.

BE IN THE ZONE

CHAPTER SEVEN

**IRONMAN: FIFTEEN HOURS FIFTEEN MINUTES
UNTIL MIDNIGHT**

I continue swimming at a strong steady pace and look up periodically to see where the next buoy is. Several hundred yards ahead of me, I can see the swimmers exiting the water. I am ready to stop swimming and begin the next stage. I end the swim strongly and, given the number of swimmers I have passed, I feel pleased with my efforts. As matters turn out, I have swum slower than I might have predicted, but given that I started the race at the end of the swimmers it has still been a good effort. I placed 12th in my age group and was 1077 among the 3050 registered athletes.

FURTHER REFLECTION

As I catch my breath, I reflect back on the year of training. The journey to complete an Ironman was an adventure in self-discovery. During the year-long odyssey of training, I learned many valuable lessons that are useful in any endeavor.

In training for the Ironman, I learned to develop a sense of pace. If I had gone out too hard, I would not have been able to complete the race. I used a heart rate monitor extensively in training. One training strategy I used was to find out what my maximum heart rate was and then back off from that to get a sustainable racing pace. I used a formula to do the calculation, but some people use actual testing. In any event, I took a pulse rate of 220 and subtracted my age to get an anaerobic threshold of 160. This would be my maximum effort for my age, which is a pace I could not keep up for long. When you race at an anaerobic pace, your body burns glucose, which is a sugar, and there is not much of this stored. The glucose is quickly depleted, and lactic acid then builds in the muscles. That is why people get so sore after a race and why many marathon runners "hit the wall." The key in long-distance racing is not to burn the glucose but instead to burn fat. Fat burning occurs at a slower, more moderate pace. The trick in going long distances is to race at a percentage of your anaerobic threshold. In order for me to race at seventy-five percent of my anaerobic threshold, I would need to hold my pulse below 140. My pulse tends to be higher when I run, so I tried to race at 135 on the bike and 140 or below on the run. If I did this, I could go forever.

People often try to go out too hard. After the first of the year, the fitness centers are always crowded. However, by July it is easy to find a machine, because the facility is empty. People begin new endeavors at a pace they cannot sustain. By running at a comfortable pace and keeping my heart rate in the proper zone, I could bike and run for hours.

At one time I had a yellow Labrador retriever named Fairfax who loved to run. I kept my running gear in our upstairs bedroom closet. When I would open the door to get out my running shoes and clothes, he would hear the door open and start to bark in wild anticipation of our run. It did not help matters that I would deliberately make a lot of noise, which just egged him on further. (I am certain my actions endeared me to my family as they tried to sleep.) On those days when I could not take him running, he would pout for hours. Weighing in excess of 100 pounds, Fairfax was strong. After I put the leash on him, he would dig in and pull me for the first part of the run. He would eventually settle down, though, and by the end of the run I was often pulling him.

Many people behave like Fairfax. They begin a race or a project with much enthusiasm, but then they fizzle. I think the reason for this is that they have not learned a sense of pace. Many of the things I have done in life have taken years to accomplish, such as becoming an Eagle Scout, going to law school or attaining a black belt in Tae Kwon Do. You have to set a goal, set milestones along the way that you celebrate when you achieve them, and pursue your goal at a sustainable pace.

In swimming we are often given a long and difficult set of repeats. To make them within the interval allowed, you have to mentally calculate your capabilities. You cannot go out too hard on the first several, because you will have nothing left for the last repeats where it becomes more difficult. You learn to develop a sense of pace and to press your capabilities but still swim within them.

I have done little biking since the Ironman. In an effort to expand my circle of friends as well as to have some camaraderie during my rides, I decided to join the Cincinnati Cycle Club. Their Saturday rides begin at a bowling alley and weave through back roads until we arrive twenty-one miles later at the small village of Pleasant Plain, where we treat ourselves to a breakfast buffet at the Plain Folks Diner. Entering the diner is like stepping back in time to the 1970s. Old albums adorn the walls, and the staff is friendly. Probably the last albums I purchased were from the 1970s, so I fit right in. Everyone looks forward to this break in the ride.

On my first ride, the leader announced that he would divide the members into three groups, based on speed and ability. Since this was only my second ride of the season, I opted for the slowest group, which would average fourteen to sixteen miles per hour. The weather was cool, and despite my lack of riding, I weaved my way toward the front and rode with the fastest riders of my group both to and from the diner. I felt good and was proud of myself.

I enjoyed the ride so much that I returned the next week. This time it was hotter. Again I started out and rode with the leaders in our group. They pushed the pace, while I struggled to stay up. Although I made it to the restaurant,

I felt fatigued from the pace. I lingered in the restaurant, enjoying the breakfast and talking to fellow bikers. When I finally left, I discovered that my group had already left. Since this was only my second experience with this group, I was unsure of the route. Fortunately, there were two others from our group who had also been left behind. They were two of the faster riders, so we decided to try to catch the main group. They took off and were almost sprinting to catch up. I fell in behind them and was glad they were breaking the wind for me.

We saw the other group in the distance and pushed to catch them. One of the other riders beckoned me to take the lead and break the wind so they could draft. I put my head down and pedaled as hard as I was able. The group was only several hundred yards away, and my two companions passed me and caught up to the other group. I was totally exhausted from this effort, and while I was within reach, I was not close enough to draft. Compounding my difficulty, there was now a strong headwind. Slowly, the group crept forward out of my reach. No matter how hard I pedaled, I could not get connected. After struggling for a while, I realized that I could not catch up with them and had to be content with fighting the headwinds by myself for the remainder of my ride.

It is no fun being dropped. Biking becomes exponentially harder, and you just have to gut it out. With ten miles left, I was exhausted and could barely complete my ride. I was spent at the conclusion of forty-two miles, and yet I realized that the Ironman would be almost triple this distance. I could not have possibly gone another seventy miles that day, despite the fact that I had done as much or more in the past. What made this particular ride so miserable?

I had worn my heart rate monitor, so after putting my bike away and collapsing in the car, I reviewed the data. My ride had taken around two hours and forty minutes, of which I spent only forty minutes in my training zone of 120-140 beats per minute. My average heart rate was 148 and my maximum was 166. That was much too high. No wonder I was spent. The difference between a ride of forty-two miles which I could barely complete and the Ironman which I completed in relative comfort was riding in the zone. As I reflect back on the Ironman race, I am thankful I had the discipline to ride within my limits and in the zone. While you may feel good for a while riding outside your limits, it takes its toll and at some point you cannot push yourself further.

The life lesson in all this is to find your limits and to work within them. This applies not just to sporting events but to anything you might attempt. Combine this approach with the thoughts in the next section, and you have a prescription for an enjoyable experience.

BUILD IN REST

CHAPTER EIGHT

IRONMAN: FOURTEEN HOURS FORTY-FIVE MINUTES UNTIL MIDNIGHT

After I exit the water, a volunteer hands me my transition bag, and I walk rapidly to the changing tent. I open my bag and pour out the contents as I notice my cut has reopened and my finger is bleeding. I dry myself, fumbling to put on my biking jersey. These jerseys are tight, and I am having trouble getting mine on. A volunteer comes over to help. As he does he asks, "How did you get blood all over your shirt?" I mutter an explanation and he helps me finish getting my gear together, and I am on my way. I grab my bike and hustle to where I can mount it. I cross that line, mount my bike and look down to reset the computer on my bike. As I do so I swerve, nearly colliding with the man next to me who was also adjusting his equipment. My race could have ended in the bike chute that day. Fortunately, we miss each other, and I am on my way.

I take a left out of the starting area and head along

the river. The first ten miles are a flat stretch of the course featuring shade trees, beautiful homes, parks, golf courses and boat slips. I check my heart rate monitor and see that it is 145. I want to keep my heart rate under 130 for the bike portion of the race. I figure it is high from the swim segment and will settle down during the flat stretch of the ride. I am playing to my heart rate and not my speed. This is like running a race looking at your tachometer, which measures the rpms of your motor rather than looking at your speedometer. I know that if I keep my heart rate at this level, I will become exhausted and be unable to continue. I need to slow down to give my body a chance to recover so I can continue. It is important to build in some rest, even in the middle of a race.

FURTHER REFLECTION

People are incredibly stressed out today. I believe part of the reason is that there is no downtime. The pace of life is brutal. My office phone has a blinking red light that tells me when I have missed a call. I am often on the phone when I see this light blinking. As soon as I hang up, retrieve the message and return the call, it seems that the light starts blinking again. Usually I am trying to multitask when I am talking on the phone. The avalanche of emails piles up, usually demanding that I provide some immediate response to an urgent request. The people who are making all these phone calls and messages are not concerned whether or not I am having a good day. On the contrary, these messages are demanding that I respond immediately to their need.

Everything is 24/7 now. With few exceptions, businesses are open seven days a week all year. Compounding this relentless pace is the fact that no matter where you go, you are bombarded by news. You cannot get away from it. Even the fast food restaurants have the news on, so you cannot even enjoy a sandwich without seeing someone being stuffed in a body bag. That certainly makes your burger taste better. The other day, I was filling up with gas when I noticed that the station had installed a new gas pump. Instead of the traditional pump which simply tells the number of gallons and amount of purchase, this one also had a miniature television which blared more news.

There is no rest built into our schedules. Our Sundays, which should be a day of rest, have become crowded with sports events and other commitments.

Even in a race, it is necessary to build in some rest. During the run, I planned on walking one minute for each four minutes I ran. On the bike portion, I stopped for five minutes at every rest stop. Granted, this cost me time in the race, but my goal was to complete the race. I was sacrificing time for rest. It turns out this was a good strategy.

It is amazing how much you can recover with just building in a little rest and allowing yourself to dream and recharge. Simply doing nothing can have tremendous therapeutic effects.

The stress in modern society and the pace of modern business stem from having to work in a compressed time frame. I believe we are bumping against the upper limits of human productivity. We try to multitask and consequently do not do anything well. I heard about a study of people who were trying to multitask, which showed that brain function underwent something akin to a brown-out, where the power is still on but not at full power supply.

Even with as many hours as were required to train for the Ironman, after a long weekend of training, Monday was designated as a day of rest. That day of rest allowed time for recovery, so I could to regain my strength and build up for the next week. Even after a particularly hard week, every third week the training program had me back off a bit to recover.

That is why God commanded us to take a day of rest. Not that God needed any rest from the creation, but he took a day of rest as an example for us. We need time to recharge our batteries. We wear out and get tired. We need to build in rest, whether it is in daily life or in training for the Ironman.

BREAK IT DOWN INTO SMALL PIECES

CHAPTER NINE

IRONMAN: FOURTEEN HOURS UNTIL MIDNIGHT

My heart rate is still elevated by the time I hit the first hill. I pass several people going up the hill and find that my hill training is paying off.

One of the major hills is now completed, but there are many more to go. After several more miles, I take a right onto KY-1694, where the next two big hills are. I reach into my supplies to take some nutrition. I have cut up two power bars into eight pieces and am scheduled to eat one every fifteen minutes. Taking nutrition is one of the most important aspects of completing the race. During the race, I will burn 500 calories per hour, and over the course of sixteen hours of effort, the amount of energy required is comparable to several days of normal activity. I have eaten three pieces so far and am getting ready to eat my fourth. It is getting hot, with temperatures probably in the high eighties by now. The piece I reach for has melted against another piece, which, in turn, has melted against the edge of the bag. I pull up the piece, and the bag comes up with it. I lose my grip, and the bag with my remaining food flies out of my hand. A major part of my food supply is now gone. I hesitate and consider turning around, but I realize this would be like trying to stop in the middle of an interstate highway during rush hour. It would not be wise, because I could cause an accident, so I continue. I will just have to rely on the food at the rest areas if I fall short.

I reluctantly leave my food in the middle of the road and continue pedaling. I concentrate on just making it to the first rest stop, which is around the twenty-five-mile mark. My strategy is to divide the race into segments and just focus on completing one leg at a time.

FURTHER REFLECTION

How do you climb a mountain? How do you handle a task that seems incredibly daunting? Attempting a big task can be overwhelming. In fact, the enormity of a quest can be so paralyzing that it keeps one from even starting it.

How do you get through this? The best way is to break down the quest into small manageable sections. For instance, in the Ironman race I broke the 2.4-mile swim into bite-size pieces. The first part of the swim route went past an island. I told myself, "I want to explore this island, so I think I will swim along it for a while and see what is on the end." When I completed that section I told myself, "Gee, there are a lot of swimmers ahead of me, and they are all heading over to that big buoy. I think I will swim over to that buoy and see what is going on." When I reached that point I said, "There is another buoy, so there must be something of interest over there. I think I will swim to the next buoy and find out." When I managed the swim in this fashion, before I knew it, that section was completed, and I was out of the water.

I handled the bike segment the same way. I first concentrated on the flat first ten miles. When that was complete, I concentrated on making it to the first rest stop where I had promised myself a break. When that was complete, I told myself to, "just make it to the town of La Grange." When I did this, I then concentrated on the second loop of the course. By breaking the race into bite-size pieces and mentally rewarding myself with small breaks when a milestone was reached, I was able to complete the race. Just break a big task into small pieces, and before you know it you will be done.

My quest for a black belt in Tae Kwon Do took over three years. Fortunately, I could complete a belt every three months. By concentrating on just making it to the next belt, I was able to make steady progress, and before I knew it, I was halfway to black belt. Once I reached the halfway point, I had too much time invested to quit.

Once I went hiking with my son Josh in the Smoky Mountains. When we planned this three-day hike, we knew we would be going up a mountain. The first day was all uphill. I figured it would become easier on the second day, but it didn't. I kept waiting for us to hit the crest of the mountain; Josh kept asking when we would start going down the hill. I kept promising him that certainly we would start down the hill just around the next bend. After two days of hiking, I could not believe we were still going uphill. When we began the third day, we were still climbing. It was only in the late afternoon of the third day that we began our descent, and it was incredibly steep. To climb this high mountain, we kept promising ourselves that surely it would get easier just around the bend. If we had known what was in store for us, we might have chosen another route, but we made it through by just taking it a step at a time.

One of my employees was diagnosed with cancer. As she informed me of the diagnosis and the looming ordeal of treatment, her eyes welled with tears and she said, "I do not think I can do this."

I asked her, "Do you think you can last through fifteen minutes of treatment?"

She pondered my question and said, "Yes, I can make it through fifteen minutes."

"Good," I replied. "Once you make it through one fifteen minute period, you can make it through the next and another fifteen minutes after that. Just focus on the fifteen minutes you are in." She confided in me later that this thought helped her immensely.

Sometimes daily life can be much more challenging than an actual race. Since the Ironman race last year, our family has been hit with a number of medical challenges. My mother-in-law opted for double-knee replacement surgery, and then there were complications, which resulted in her spending time in the intensive care unit. At the same time, my father had an infection in his toe, and part of his toe had to be amputated. Added to the mix were challenges facing our teenaged son, which went beyond the normal growing pains of adolescence. All of this, combined with my fast-paced work environment, made me just want to crawl into a corner somewhere and assume the fetal position. My wife commented that we just needed to take it day by day. That goes with the life lesson in breaking it down into small pieces. When life seems overwhelming, just break it down into small pieces.

TRAIN FOR TIME, NOT DISTANCE

CHAPTER TEN

IRONMAN: THIRTEEN HOURS UNTIL MIDNIGHT

I complete one long hill on Ky-1694, and several miles later there is the turnaround where I ride down the hill I just climbed. The ride down is sure a lot faster than the climb up. Once I complete the downhill, another big hill looms ahead. While coming up the second hill, I see my first ambulance of the day. A woman lies sprawled by the side of the road. She is not moving, which is not a good sign. In confirmation of my thoughts, I notice the EMS officials looking on with concern. She apparently lost control of her bike and hit a wooden post which keeps cars from going into a creek if they lose control. She must have hit the post with considerable impact, since it is now tilted at an odd angle. I continue my climb and hope I will be safe for the balance of the ride.

I stop at the rest stop to refill my water bottle and then continue on. Through the first twenty-three miles, I hold a pace of sixteen miles per hour. That is fast, considering I have just ridden three of the toughest hills in the course. My heart rate has settled down after the rest stop, and I am determined to keep it there for the remainder of the race. After KY-1694, I travel through beautiful horse country and incredible farms stretching as far as the eye can see. My pace for the next seventeen miles slows considerably to fourteen miles per hour. I must be enjoying the scenery. I try to concentrate on keeping a steady pace, knowing I will have to keep myself going for the next thirteen hours. I am prepared for this, because I have trained to keep a steady pace for a long time.

FURTHER REFLECTION

Time management is one of the most important lessons I learned during my training for the Ironman. If you are incredibly busy, how do you manage your time? Here is the answer: Train for time and not for distance. If you have only an hour to do a run, just run for one hour. Do not get stressed about covering a particular distance. Some days you feel better than others. Why compound your discomfort by trying to cover too much distance on your off days?

One day I was talking with a friend, and he asked how far I had gone on my bike the day before. I said, "I rode for four and a half hours." He looked at me strangely. "You mean you didn't calculate your mileage?" I told him I knew how far I had ridden, but my focus was on time and not mileage. By focusing on time, you can build a workout around whatever time you have available.

I used this technique extensively during my year of training. When my niece got married, I drove to the East Coast to attend the wedding. I got to the hotel, and after checking in, I had only about an hour and a half before dinner. I quickly got into my workout clothes and ran for an hour around the hotel and adjacent streets. I did not worry about the distance I covered, but since I had only an hour to work with, that is what I used.

The next day I did the same thing. This time I ran for an hour and a half and found some nice surprises along the way. I dodged strollers and families as I ran through a Greek festival, and I turned around at the beautiful harbor. Since I am from Ohio, this is something I do not generally get to see. Use the time you have available, and don't worry about the distance.

This will work for anything. I purchased the book *Piano for Dummies*, and I am working my way through it, trying to practice for half an hour per day. If I can keep this pace up for one year I should be able to nail "Chopsticks" or even "On Top of Old Smokey." By just practicing one half hour per day over the course of a year, I will have devoted a working month to practice, calculated as forty hours per week for four weeks. Practicing in half-hour increments is better than trying to practice for an hour and a half after missing several days. I begin to lose my concentration after a half hour anyway, so for me to practice longer becomes counterproductive.

You can apply this to anything, such as learning a second language or writing a book. I am using this technique to write this book. I write for half an hour a day and then stop. Think of all the time that is wasted during the day. If we could focus just a little of that time into another endeavor, imagine what we might accomplish!

DO SOMETHING

CHAPTER ELEVEN

**IRONMAN: ELEVEN HOURS FORTY-FIVE MINUTES
UNTIL MIDNIGHT**

When I enter the town of La Grange, the streets are packed with cheering people, and I enjoy waving to them as I pass. I look for my family but still do not see them. Once outside of La Grange, I begin to be passed by athletes who are now completing their second lap. I am in awe of how fast they can move on their bikes.

My pace for the next thirty miles slows considerably, not so much because I am riding slowly, but because I choose to take my time at the water stops. Riding an endless string of rolling hills is taking it out of me, so when I come to a water stop, I take a break for several minutes. I drink a full bottle of water and eat one of the energy bars that are offered and sometimes even a banana. By the third water stop, I am beginning to feel woozy, as if I might be becoming dehydrated, which could quickly end my race. I guzzle a bottle of water and then ask for another. After drinking the second bottle, I feel much better. The water stops take time, but I want to make sure I have the right hydration and nutrition, otherwise I will not be able to finish. I will myself to keep moving toward the finish. I am doing something.

FURTHER REFLECTION

For many people, it is easy to procrastinate and do nothing, never moving toward their goal. Therefore it is important to begin to take steps toward your goal. The steps do not need to be large, but they need to proceed in a positive direction. I often notice stickers on cars. The other day, I saw a sticker which said "13.1," which means that someone ran a half-marathon. That is a tremendous accomplishment! The individual who has this sticker had to set a goal and train to achieve it. For them, this is probably the farthest they have ever run. To have completed this feat is quite an achievement, and the person has the right to be proud of this accomplishment.

If you have been sedentary, do not start with a half marathon, but rather begin with a 5k. The important thing is just to begin. In other words, do something. Begin where you are, and you can move forward from there.

By taking small steps, you can be successful. Once you achieve the small steps, you have time and energy invested, which makes it harder to quit. In this way, small steps lead to success.

Cincinnati has a race in the spring called the Heart Mini-marathon. It is a 15k race, and I remember the first time I ran it. I did not know how to train, but I was thirty years younger then. Because the race was held in the early spring, it was cold that day. In fact, there were snow flurries. I kept thinking that since there were snow flurries, surely they would call off the race, which shows you how little I knew.

I dressed in several layers of clothes, and my outfit was more appropriate for leading a dog team on an assault to the South Pole than running the race. When I got downtown, I ran into one of my friends who is at the top of his age group; the only thing he said while shaking his head was, "You will get really hot the way you are dressed." Of course, he was right. I did not know any better. I completed the race and learned from my experience that during a race you heat up. It is best to be cold at the beginning of the race, because surely by the end you will be hot.

I began with this race and have competed in many races since. As I raced more, I gained confidence, until finally I completed several marathons. The important lesson is that you need to begin. Begin somewhere, but just begin.

The law of inertia in physics states that a body at rest will remain at rest. A body in motion will tend to remain in motion. Therefore, you need to get your body in motion, and the best way to do that is just to begin. You will also find that once you begin toward a goal, you want to keep the momentum going. You will have too much time invested to quit. I dread missing several days of swimming. I find that even after only a few days off, I begin to lose conditioning, and the workouts are much more difficult.

WELCOME SURPRISES

CHAPTER TWELVE

IRONMAN: TEN AND ONE HALF HOURS UNTIL MIDNIGHT

It is during the second lap of the bike segment that the hills and the heat begin to extract a terrible toll on the racers. The temperature is now in the nineties, with humidity to match. Few clouds provide relief. I am baking. There is no wind, and the air is still. The only breeze I have to cool me off is from the speed of my own bike. I feel the sweat pouring off my head, running down my cheeks and onto my arms and soaking my gloves. I become increasingly concerned about the loss of fluids and the risk of dehydration. In confirmation of my fears, I see increasing numbers of bikers dismounting and lying under trees, trying to recover. Ambulances abound, treating athletes with heat exhaustion. I am reminded of what it must have felt like on those wagon trains traveling out West, seeing the remains of an abandoned wagon or the skeleton of an animal. I know all too well that it could be me lying under some tree, unable to continue. I keep reminding myself to drink fluids; however, my water bottles are now nearly empty, and I do not know how far it is to the next rest stop. I have to pace my fluid intake until then and hope I have enough to make it. The racers are spread out, and we are now on the second fifty-six miles. I am on my own and feeling lonely. Before the race, I was advised that the race will not always go according to plan. You have to adjust and embrace the change.

FURTHER REFLECTION

Not everything in life goes as planned. You will find many surprises along the way. About a month out from my Ironman race, I was vacationing in Michigan. I was using my "vacation" to do some long workouts. My plan was to attempt a full Ironman 112-mile bike ride one day, and then the next day to run for five hours, which would put me close to a full marathon. On the day of my bike ride, I got up early and was on the road by 7:00, when it was light enough that cars could see me. I started from our cottage in Union Pier and headed toward Michigan City, which was a distance of around fifteen miles. I arrived in Michigan City and found traffic was light. While weaving through the streets, I slowed at a stop sign. When I went to switch gears to increase my speed, I began to pedal but felt my chain slip. I had no traction. I tried to unclip from my pedals, but it was too late. I fell hard and heard several bike parts rattle into the street. I was still attached to my bike after I fell, and I struggled to unclip myself with my bike still on top of me. After I freed myself from the bike,

I examined it for damage and saw the back derailleur was bent and contorted into an unworkable position. I picked up the parts from the street and saw a spoke was also broken from the back wheel. I realized my ride was over. I called Stu, who fortunately had a meeting in the area and also had his bike with him. Ironically, I fell right by the hospital, so if I had injured myself I could have staggered into the emergency room.

Stu loaded my bike into his car and was gracious enough to allow me to use his bike for the balance of the ride. Fortunately, I was able to complete what I had set out to do. Stu rescued me, and had it not been for him, I would not have been able to complete this critical training ride. (No wonder I dedicated this race to Stu.)

Stu took my bike in for repair, and he called me mid-afternoon to see where I was. I gave him directions, and we met and completed the final twenty miles together.

Following these repairs, the trials with my bike continued. A week after returning home, I had planned to do a two-hour bike ride to East Fork Lake. I got my bike ready, filled my water bottles and pedaled off. I took a right turn out of my driveway, which is downhill, and built up speed to twenty-five miles per hour. When I began to shift gears to pedal uphill, I felt something give in my chain. I was pedaling, but nothing was happening. Fortunately, this time I was able to unclip in time to avoid falling. I inspected the damage and discovered my chain had broken. This ended my planned bike ride for that day.

I walked my bike home and instead ran for an hour.

My suspicion was that I had weakened the chain when I had fallen the week before. Perhaps there was a greater purpose in all this sequence of events, which I was glad was happening now, and not during the race! I had time to get things fixed, which I would not have had during the race. God is sovereign, and if He knows when a bird falls out of a tree, certainly He knew when my chain was about to break. Perhaps these setbacks all happened when they did so that I could make the repairs needed to complete the race.

Stu and me before a bike ride.

Family support is critical to complete an Ironman.

Front row (left to right): My daughter Emily and my son Sam. Back row (left to right): Emily's husband Nathan, my wife Gretchen, me, and my son Josh.

Lining up for the swim segment, officially beginning my Giant Journey.

Completing one of the many climbs on the bike route.

Photo Credit: FinisherPix.com

Baking on the bridge. With temperatures in the 90s, the bridge was like a griddle.
Photo Credit: FinisherPix.com

Crossing the finish line with just minutes to spare.

Photo Credit: FinisherPix.com

Stu providing much-needed encouragement during the race.

A huge smile of relief after finishing.

NEVER QUIT

CHAPTER THIRTEEN

IRONMAN: NINE HOURS UNTIL MIDNIGHT

Somewhere along the second lap, athletes can retrieve a "special needs bag," packed with extra food and beverages. I had considered packing a "special needs bag," but opted instead to carry everything I might need so I would not have to make another stop, losing valuable time looking for my bag among the thousands of other bags. As matters turn out, this was a good decision. After I pass the "special needs bag" pick-up area, I see a biker passing me. He provides me with some comic relief, as I see him balancing a Subway sandwich between his handlebars. "You have a virtual buffet on your bike," I call to him as he passes. He laughs and says, "I know! I just have not figured out how I will eat it." He continues pedaling past me, and somehow he must have found a way to finish his sandwich.

The bikers are now spread out, and there is not much company. I am alone with my thoughts. The thought of quitting does not enter my mind. I remember Stu's ordeal and how he never quit. At this point, they will have to drag me off the course in a stupor before I stop.

STU'S JOURNEY

The gift of continued life has turned Stu into a perpetual motion machine. After the bike ride I wrote about earlier, I went to the beach and was just content to lie in my chair soaking up the sun while I took a nap. While I was napping, Stu rigged up the sailboat, played catch with my son, and was busy trying to induce everyone to swim to a far buoy through three foot waves. At the end of the day, he usually just collapses in a chair in front of the television.

At this point in his life, Stu needs to have both hips replaced because of all his medical treatments. I know he is in considerable pain, because he gets stiff at the end of the day and has trouble walking. Most people would be doubled over from the pain, but somehow Stu continues. He presses on day by day and extracts all the beauty and wonder life has to offer. He is not a quitter.

FURTHER REFLECTION

My friend Shawn, who is a member of our Masters Swim Team, has also completed an Ironman. I asked him what was the most important advice he could give me and he said simply, "Never quit." That was it, just two words, but they made a big impact.

Business had been awful for the past seven years, but last year it turned. Interest rates dropped, and we became profitable. If I had become discouraged and quit when things were dark, I never would have enjoyed the moment when things changed.

You can see this happen time and time again in sports. One team will often gain an initial lead that at the time seems insurmountable. However, the other team keeps trying and simply doesn't quit. Then there is a play that is the turning point of the game, and the momentum shifts. The team that didn't quit comes back and wins.

The life lesson in all this is to keep trying, never give up and never quit, because your fortune will eventually turn.

DRESS REHEARSAL

CHAPTER FOURTEEN

IRONMAN: EIGHT HOURS UNTIL MIDNIGHT

At this point, I am midway through my second lap. I have completed the first lap and know what to expect for the balance of the bike ride, which is endless rolling hills. However, the beauty of the Kentucky horse country provides a welcome distraction. I look back on my training year and contemplate what I could have done differently to train for this event.

It is ironic that I trained for the race, ignoring the advice I am about to give. This is what I tell my kids: "Do as I say and not as I do." There is nothing like living a consistent life. The best way to simulate race conditions is to schedule several races before the big race. Everything I read recommended that I compete in an Olympic distance event and one half Ironman before my big day. Unfortunately, my only race in 2012 was the Ironman competition itself. We had a busy schedule, filled with weddings and other activities, so I was never able to do a practice race. It certainly would have helped.

That is why they have dress rehearsals in plays. It enables you to work out the kinks. Had I completed several practice races, I am sure I could have improved on how I was taking my nutrition and hydration, and I would have found a way to improve my transition times. I also would have had a better sense of how long the race was going to take. I could have done a better job of predicting my race performance and might not have cut my timing so close.

FURTHER REFLECTION

Several years ago, I went with my dad to visit New Zealand. In the southern island, we saw a statue of Sir Edmund Hillary, who was the first person to successfully climb Mt. Everest. His statue overlooked a large mountain in the Southern Alps, where he practiced his climbing techniques. It was on this mountain that he refined the craft that would ultimately take him to the summit of the earth's tallest mountain.

In any endeavor, you need to simulate as best you can the conditions under which you will perform. That is why so many of the athletes actually rode the course ahead of time. They wanted to know what to expect. Once you do this, it is easier to plan and prepare. Schedule a dress rehearsal, and your actual performance will be much smoother.

IMPROVISE

CHAPTER FIFTEEN

.

**IRONMAN: SEVEN AND ONE HALF HOURS
UNTIL MIDNIGHT**

Math is difficult in the middle of the race, even simple calculations. The brain simply does not function well under race conditions. I try to calculate how much margin I have according to the Ironman cut-off times. I had two and a half hours after the last swimmer entered the water to complete the swim. I know I was one of the last swimmers in the water, and know I made this cut-off by a wide margin of over an hour. The second lap of the bike had to be started by 2:20 p.m. While I am not overly concerned, I am beginning to lose my bearings. My watch is set to calculate my race time and not to display the time of day. I could try to adjust it, but I do not want to push the wrong button and stop my race time. I feel that I am doing fine, but I am not sure.

I finally locate my wife, my daughter Emily and my son Sam, along with Barb and Stu, on my second lap of the bike. They are in the town of La Grange, which provides good visibility for watching the bikers. I spot them in the crowd and stop to visit for a while. That is my excuse to rest. My family rebuffs my visit and says, "You had better not stop; keep going!" I hook my feet back into my pedals and continue on. They know what I do not. They have made the calculation that I need to push ahead to make sure I am under the deadline. They know what I do not: how close I am to the cut-off time. If I had actually known this, it would have thrown me into a sense of panic.

Fortunately, I have yet to encounter any major disasters during the race. So far I have not had a flat tire or fallen off my bike. I have not gone too fast down a hill and crashed like the one racer I saw. The only minor setback was when I dropped some of my food. Sometimes you are fortunate, and other times things happen. On those occasions when something happens, you have to improvise.

FURTHER REFLECTION

My son Josh is a Captain in the Air Force. My family and I visited Josh while he was training at Beale Air Force Base in California to fly the MC12, which is a retrofitted King Air commercial plane now used by the Air Force to perform reconnaissance duties. We knew he would be deployed by the year's end, so we wanted to visit him at his new assignment. He lives in Rocklin, California, which is a paradise. During our visit, there was hardly a cloud in the sky, and temperatures were in the seventies, which made for a nice change from the heat and humidity in

Cincinnati. I did not expect to do any biking or swimming while we were there, so I had been doing extra running instead. I ran before breakfast and devised various routes through different neighborhoods. One day we drove to Lake Tahoe, which is truly one of the most beautiful places on earth. Josh and I walked up a steep mountain to get a better view of the lake. Not only was the mountain steep, but we quickly got winded because the elevation was over 6000 feet. I realized that I was not always getting in the workouts I had planned, but by staying flexible, I was enjoying the training. By improvising and staying flexible, you too may even be able to train with your son in Lake Tahoe.

The other bit of improvising I did on the trip was in swimming. For some reason, I brought my swim suit and goggles, just in case I could find a pool. I looked in the phone book and found a public pool near the hotel. I called to see if I could get a membership for one day, and sure enough, they said I could. So I got up early the next day to get in one swim workout. The workout was great, but I was surprised to find out that they did not furnish towels. So again, I improvised and used my shirt for a towel.

Improvising unleashes the creative energy in you as you seek solutions to problems. Remember the movie *Apollo 13*, when the astronauts had to improvise and create a piece of equipment to save their lives? Now, that is performance under pressure!

YOU CAN DO MORE
THAN YOU THINK

CHAPTER SIXTEEN

**IRONMAN: SIX HOURS AND FORTY-FIVE MINUTES
UNTIL MIDNIGHT**

The citizens of Louisville provide great support throughout the race. The volunteers will do anything I ask at the rest stops and the residents spend the day camped by the side of the road, shouting encouragement as the athletes ride past. They are an inspiration.

I pick up the pace a little on the second lap, completing the last forty miles at 13.5 miles per hour. My total time on the bike is eight hours and six minutes. By the time I dismount my bike, I have been racing for nine hours and forty-three minutes. I am fifteen minutes off where I think I ought to be. At this point, I have already exceeded my longest training day, and I am pushing the boundaries of what I think I can do.

FURTHER REFLECTION

When my son Josh was in his third year at the Air Force Academy, his class was responsible for training the incoming class of cadets. The training is rigorous, and the cadets are pushed to their limits. Josh told me about one drill they had the incoming class perform, which was to lie on their backs and do flutter kicks. This exercise can take its toll on stomach muscles after only several hundred kicks. The exercise commenced, and soon the class had done 500 flutter kicks. They kept going. Soon they passed 1,000 kicks. This continued until they passed 1,500 kicks. By then the class thought they knew the number of kicks they would stop at. Since Josh was training the class of 2012, they naturally assumed they would stop at 2,012 kicks. They didn't, and the exercise continued. Finally, at 2,500 kicks the exercise stopped. Josh just smiled as he recalled that day and said, "By the end they were just lying on the ground twitching." The life lesson in all of this is that you can do more than you think you can. I doubt that prior to that day any member of the class had ever done more than several hundred of these kicks. I also doubt that at the beginning of the exercise any thought they were capable of accomplishing what they did. Every member of that class had exceeded by far what they thought they could accomplish.

I know that when I first started learning Tae Kwon Do, the idea of breaking a brick with my bare hand was inconceivable. After several years of practicing on breaking boards with increasing thickness, I was finally ready.

So much of what you can do is in your head. I never thought of quitting during the Ironman race. I just told myself that no matter how hot it was or how bad I felt, I would keep going until someone pulled me off the course and forced me to stop.

THE EYE OF THE TIGER

CHAPTER SEVENTEEN

IRONMAN: SIX AND ONE HALF HOURS UNTIL MIDNIGHT

Now the race is beginning to take its toll. I take my time after the bike leg of the race to get ready for the run. I remember the words of one of my friends who had completed the Ironman. He said, "After the bike ride I felt like quitting and almost did. I took a couple of minutes rest. I decided to put on my shoes, and then started to run. By then I was beginning to feel better, so I was able to complete the race."

Based on his experience, I am prepared to feel bad after the bike portion. I have placed a drink in my transition bag, but it tastes awful since it has been under the hot sun all day. After fifteen minutes or so, I exit the tent, apply some sunscreen and see Emily and Stu, who want to track with me for a little of the running course. I plan to walk for a mile or so to give myself a chance to get hydrated before beginning the run. Stu walks with us for several blocks, and Emily accompanies me onto the bridge. The bridge, which crosses from Louisville into

Indiana, has been baking under the ninety-plus degrees sunless sky for hours, so it is more appropriate at that moment for grilling waffles than for hosting runners. I want to get out of that oven before beginning the run. The drink I had at the transition area is not sitting well, so I throw up in the middle of the bridge. I put on a nice display for my daughter. Emily keeps saying, "You can do this, Dad." I then tell her I am ready to begin my run. I start by running for one minute and walking another. My legs are still stiff from the bike ride, and I am having trouble getting moving. I feel like I am running on tree stumps. After several minutes, I pick up my running to two minutes for every minute of walking. Finally, I feel like my legs are coming back, so I pick up the pace to four minutes of running for every minute of walking. I find that I can do several rounds of this but still have to insert additional walk breaks.

The temperature is still scorching. At this point, it is just a matter of trying to survive until the sun goes down and the evening gets cooler. In the interim, I just need to cover as much ground as possible until sunset. I know Stu and my family are rooting for me, and I cannot let them down. I have to keep moving.

STU'S JOURNEY

Stu has not only been an inspiration to me, but he has also inspired others to do more than they thought possible. He has handled the trials of his illness with a quiet dignity that others see. The way in which he tackled his problems has inspired others to dig in and persevere in their own trials. One of his friends, Tony, is a gifted biker, and he signed up for the Leadville 100, which is a difficult race in Colorado that entails pedaling up a steep mountain. It is one thing to climb a hill and look forward to a nice downhill to rest. It is a totally different effort when the race consists of an uphill climb at high altitude for the whole race. When Tony reached the point of the race when he could not continue, he thought of Stu and all Stu had been through. He thought, "If Stu can get through his treatment, then I can continue." Tony had developed the eye of the tiger using Stu's example.

FURTHER REFLECTION

During the course of training, there were several tough workouts that helped sharpen me for the race. I remember one run in particular. I had planned a three-hour training run, but the weather forecast called for rain. Fortunately, it was warm that day, so I dressed in a light running jacket. As I left my garage, I felt the beginning of a few sprinkles. "This is not bad," I thought, as I continued down our street. I rounded the corner, and the rain picked up slightly. By the time I had completed one mile, it was raining hard. "Surely, this will stop soon," I told myself. It didn't. In fact, the rain increased in intensity and soaked my running jacket. Although I was soaked, I was still relatively warm, so I continued. This continued on into the first hour of my run, and as I started the second hour. I was several miles from home by this time, so even if I had wanted to stop, it would have taken me some time to get home.

By the third hour of the run, there was not one inch of dry skin on me. My shoes were drenched as I ran through the giant puddles. My wife was expecting me home, and I am sure she was thinking, "No one would be crazy enough to continue in this," so she called me. I reached for my phone, having trouble getting it out of my jacket and sliding the bar to answer it. "Where are you?" she asked with obvious concern. "I am still running, "I replied. "I will be home in half an hour." I completed my workout and was pleased that I was able to continue through the bad weather.

In the movie *Rocky III*, one of the theme songs is "The Eye of the Tiger" by the American rock band Survivor. When you complete a tough workout and spend many months focusing and training for an event, you develop the eye of the tiger. You develop a focused determination to complete the task no matter what. You have too much time and energy invested to think of quitting. You just want to bring it on.

One Saturday in early April, I scheduled a seventy-five-mile bike ride, which was to be the longest I had ridden up to that point. I was going to ride the tough hills around East Fork Lake, but given that rain was predicted, I opted for the safety of the Loveland Bike Trail. I rode from Newtown to Loveland, a distance of fourteen miles, and stopped for a brief rest. I noticed a father with his son, studying his cell phone intently. I asked him if he was checking the weather, and he said there was a major band of showers heading our way. I would be fine if I turned around. Still, I wanted to get my seventy-five miles in, so I opted to go on. Everything went smoothly until I turned around at thirty-seven miles. Then the heavens opened up. I had trouble seeing on account of the blinding rain. The rain continued for the next several hours, soaking through my windbreaker and clothes. By the time I got back to Loveland for another brief stop, I was shaking so hard I could not even remove my helmet. I finally managed to rip it from my head, so I could go to the restroom. The rain abated somewhat, and then with seven miles to go, as if to taunt me, the heavens opened up again. I finally made it back, cold and miserable, but satisfied that I had endured an incredibly uncomfortable training ride. All this builds mental toughness for the race. I rewarded myself with a nice warm soaking bath when I got home.

I had another memorable workout, so humor me as I recount the experience. I signed up for a 100-mile bike ride with the Cincinnati Cycle Club. The longest distance I had ever attempted before that ride was seventy-five miles, which was the ride in the rain on the Loveland Bike Trail. Since the Ironman bike segment is 112 miles, I wanted to know how it feels to ride 100 miles at one time.

My understanding was that organized groups would depart from Goshen High School at 7:00 a.m. and ride at a particular pace. However, when I got there, someone told me that you just start and ride the course; there would always be someone to ride with.

After getting my bike ready, I began to ride and caught up with two younger men. I tried to engage them in conversation but they did not say much. I thought, "This sure is going to be a fun 100 miles." I am sure they were thinking, "How can we ditch this old geezer who is asking annoying questions we have to answer?" After several miles, we caught up with several other riders, and things began to improve. They would at least talk to me. Two of them rode on a consistent basis with the Cincinnati Cycle Club, and I was able to discuss the club with them. We rode and talked for several more miles, and then I heard a noise like a car behind me. I was about to cry out, "Car back," when a group of around thirty cyclists began to pass us. I quickly gave chase, determined to see how long I could keep up with them. I fell in around three-fourths of the way back. One lesson I quickly learned was that having someone ride ahead and break the air makes a big difference. We were riding nineteen to twenty-two miles per hour. That is flying for me. I am lucky to hold a sixteen to seventeen mile per hour average when riding alone. I managed to hold with them until the first rest stop at twenty-five miles. After resting, eating bagels with peanut butter and a banana and refilling our water bottles, we began again. I held tough until mile forty, when we hit a slight hill, and I fell behind. It was over by then. Here is another lesson I learned. When you fall behind and out of the stream where someone is breaking the wind resistance ahead of you, it is all over. I never could catch up. After mile forty, I was able to keep a pace of only eighteen and a half miles per hour.

I rode alone until the next rest stop, when I found the guys I was riding with earlier. We decided to ride together, and by alternating leaders, we were able to hold a fast steady pace. We rode together until mile seventy-five, when they called it a day. As of mile seventy-five, my average pace had been eighteen miles per hour. I began to ride the final twenty-five miles by myself. The route was adequately marked, but you had to be careful or you would miss a turn. I passed a rider who had stopped by the side of the road and asked if he was all right. He said he was, and I continued on. Several miles later he caught up with me, and after exchanging a few words, he sped ahead. I decided to follow him, since he looked like he knew the way home. That proved to be a mistake. I lost sight of him and could not find any of the markers for the route. I could not find what road I was on using the map I had been provided. Fortunately, I had my smart phone with me, so I input my destination, which was Goshen High School, and began to rely on the voice from the phone to guide me. The voice kept reassuring me that there were just several miles to go. That was good, because I was running out of water and I was hot. Finally, I cruised into town, but it was the wrong town. I was not in Goshen at all! My phone had directed me to Owensville, which not only was ten miles from my destination, but the town also happened to be in the midst of a city-wide garage sale. Traffic was backed up on every road, and people with kids were cluttering the sidewalk. I picked my way through them and realized here I was at mile ninety-seven, and I still had a long way to Goshen. If that weren't enough, there is a steep hill outside of Goshen which I still had to climb. That took several minutes, and after alternating between sitting on the seat and standing on my pedals I made it to the top. Finally, after 107 miles, I finished my journey. Despite the extra mileage and picking my way through Owensville, I managed to hold a pace throughout of seventeen and a quarter miles per hour. The total rolling time to cover this mileage was six hours and eleven minutes. I treated myself to a couple of Cheese Coneys following the ride, courtesy of the Cincinnati Cycle Club.

Here are some life lessons from that day: First, you can do more than you think you can. I covered over twenty-five percent more distance than I had ever done previously. Second, once you separate yourself from the pack, it is over. Third, it feels great to get in shape. Fourth, a long ride like this helped to instill confidence that I could complete the Ironman. You remember these tough workouts, and when you are hurting in the race, you remind yourself of what you have been through, the investments in time and agony. Then you press forward.

Several years ago, my in-laws treated my wife and me to an Alaskan cruise. Often these cruises have guest lecturers. In one port we were treated to a lecture by Libby Riddles, who became the first woman to win the Iditarod dog sled race. The Iditarod dog sled race is not only grueling in its length, which stretches a distance of 1200 miles from Anchorage to Nome, Alaska, but during the course of this multi-day race the participants face blizzards, extreme cold and exhaustion. Sometimes the temperatures reach fifty-two degrees below zero. She told many stories about her adventures along the way. I listened in amazement, grateful that all my races are in a warmer climate.

In addition to the physical challenges, there are challenges from the wild animals. Early in the race, Libby was not in the lead. One of the leaders stumbled upon a moose. Moose are known for their poor eyesight. Thinking that the dog team converging on it was a pack of wolves, the terrified moose killed several of the dogs and left the musher bruised, dazed and out of the race. This is not a race for the faint of heart.

At the end of each grueling day Libby had to feed her dogs, which she did first before feeding herself. She had to take an ax and cut a slab of frozen meat from the provisions in her sled. She then had to build a fire and cook the meat. At least the Ironman is a one-day event, and afterwards I could treat myself to a hot shower and a nice warm bed. Riddles did not have this luxury; she had to pitch a tent after each hard day of sledding.

Deep into the race, Libby took a huge gamble. A raging blizzard pinned the other dog teams down. She decided to keep racing despite the blizzard. She and her team somehow managed to navigate through a long stretch of trackless sea ice. Feeling lost and as if she were just traveling in circles, she endured winds in excess of fifty miles per hour. One of the other racers commented that, "The wind was blowing like it was directed at us with a fire hose. We went until the dogs quit. One after another, our teams quit. The dogs would do only so much in that wind." Riddles, however, pressed on.

By continuing on when others could not, Riddles gained enough of an advantage to allow her to become the first woman to win this race. Sometimes you have to take some chances, and by having gone through prior difficulties, you develop the eye of the tiger, which enables you to push beyond your limits.

GROW WHERE YOU ARE PLANTED

CHAPTER EIGHTEEN

IRONMAN: FOUR HOURS UNTIL MIDNIGHT

My plan is to do what I can for the first thirteen miles and pray it gets cooler when the sun goes down. I continue to bake as I run, since the temperature is in the high eighties. I know the first lap needs to be completed by 9:25, so if I can make this time, perhaps it will be easier on the second lap.

The course is flat, and I find many runners have adopted the strategy I am using, either by design or by necessity. They run some and then walk some. Around eight miles out of the city is a turnaround, and then the course takes you back into the heart of the city to complete the first lap. It is now getting dark. Stu is concerned about my pace and location and sets out to look for me on his bike. He finds me walking again at the ten mile mark. At this point I am in trouble, the kind of deep dark trouble that borders on disaster. Stu rolls up beside me. He quickly recognizes that I am in trouble, because I am not saying anything. He is right. I am out of gas and running on fumes, with sixteen miles still to go. Now I really feel like quitting, but Stu says something that changes the outcome of the race for me.

He tells me this story with slow, deliberate words, designed to register with me: "When I received my bone marrow transplant, I did not know whether I would live or die. My doctor told me if I was to live, I had to get on my bike and ride. One day I did not feel like doing this. I felt sick and just did not want to get out of bed. My doctor stuck his head in my door and commanded, 'Stu, get on your bike and ride.' I had to decide what I would do then. I could continue to lie in bed and perhaps not make it, or I could get out of my bed and ride my bike. After lying there for a while, I made my decision. I got out of bed, got on my bike and rode."

Stu then concludes, "If you are going to make this, you have to run. So start running." He then pedals away into the darkness, letting his words sink in and leaving me with my thoughts. Somewhere in the recesses of my consciousness this registers, and I begin to run again. While I am not the fastest triathlete, I have to do the best I can with the gifts I have been given.

FURTHER REFLECTION

When I was completing a draft of this book, I had a discussion with Tim Mettey, who is the Chief Executive Officer of Matthew 25: Ministries. I commented,

"Normally a book of this sort is written by the winner of the race, who was so good that he finishes fifteen minutes ahead of the nearest competitor. My book is about some guy who just barely finishes the race before the deadline."

Tim thought about my comments for a moment and offered the following: "That may be true, but many people are barely keeping their heads above water. They are experiencing financial problems, loss of family and jobs, and a life of trouble. They may be able to relate more to your book than to a book by the winner." His comments hit home. We all need to make the most of what we have.

Many years ago, I took a business trip to San Francisco. I had some time to kill before my flight back home, so I took a drive along the rugged California coast. There is a route called the seventeen-mile drive, which hugs the coast. During the course of the ride you are treated to views of stately mansions, the famous Pebble Beach Golf Course, and sea lions sunning themselves on rocks. When I went to view the sea lions I noticed some cute squirrels that lived among the rocks on the shore. Several years later, my wife and I celebrated our anniversary in the same area. I told her about this beautiful drive, and we set out to enjoy it together.

When we went to the area where the sea lions were, after leaving the car, I again noticed the rock squirrels. I proceeded to impress my wife by making happy squirrel noises, trying to induce a squirrel to come near. It worked. One squirrel was curious and thought I was offering it food. It then proceeded to jump on my leg. I could feel its claws go through my pants and it proceeded to climb up the leg of my pants. I was startled and jumped, and it jumped, too. This commotion caused his buddies to think that I was offering food, and a pack of squirrels began to chase us back to our car.

The scene was reminiscent of the scene from Alfred Hitchcock's horror movie *The Birds* where a monstrous flock of ravens harasses a town, only in this case, my wife and I were chased by a pack of hungry squirrels which were ticked off because I did not feed them.

The rest of our journey was more sedate. We did make a stop at a much-photographed site. Alone at the end of a rock stands a tree. While there are many trees in the woods, this tree is unique. This tree has been captured in many photographs of the area. There is hardly any soil on which the tree can grow. Its roots cling to the stark hard rock. There is nothing to protect it from the cold and salty sea breeze. It stands at the edge of a rock overlooking the sea in defiance of all that nature throws at it. What attracts people to this tree is that it has grown despite all the formidable obstacles it faces. This tree has grown where it is planted. It has grown and thrived despite its adverse conditions. You can often make a greater impact on people when they realize not so much what you have accomplished but what you have overcome.

Initially, I had intended to co-author this book with my friend Debbie, a gifted swimmer who swims in my lane on our Seawolves Masters Swim Team. She and her son Matthew hiked the tallest mountain in Africa, Mt. Kilimanjaro, and dedicated their journey to one of Matthew's classmates who was battling cancer. Her cancer was in remission at the time, and they thought it would be appropriate to dedicate their climb to her and to raise money for cancer research. The climb was successful, and following their return the news media picked up the story of their climb. When they returned, they were also saddened to learn that their friend's cancer had returned. When I asked Debbie about co-authoring the book, she demurred and said something that still resonates with me. "For some people, just being able to put one foot in front of the other is their giant journey." Indeed, her friend's struggle to come back after the recurrence of cancer is a lesson in making the best of what life has dealt you.

That is what I admire so much about Stu. Despite his battle with cancer, liver transplant, hepatitis, and now degenerative hips, he still rides his bike, embraces each day and makes the best of his life. He has grown where he has been planted. People see this, and they admire his attitude. People look at Stu and admire what he has overcome. That is the true victory.

Following the Ironman competition, I composed a bucket list of things I want to do during the next several years. One of my wishes was to appear in the movies. I have always wanted to be an extra in a scene with a panicked crowd, preferably as some monster or invading army creates havoc on a city. I can hear myself crying, "Run, Godzilla, run," as I sprint to safety.

I got my big break recently. One of my friends started a film production company right here in Cincinnati. Cincinnati is not exactly a mecca for film production. It is not Hollywood or New York, but my friend persevered anyway. His vision is to produce faith-based films which inspire and contain a moral message. He is producing a film about the first century Christian martyr Polycarp, so I signed up to be an extra. They accepted my application because they need older, mature men in the movie. Once I checked in to the set, I was directed to the wardrobe department, where they outfitted me in first-century garb. They put make-up on my face and even sprayed my feet to make them look dirty. The last stop was the hairstylist. I asked if they could braid my hair like the girl ahead of me, and they politely ushered me along, since I am nearly bald.

After a long wait, I was finally called for my big scene. I was cast as a creepy fish vendor. I had to act as if I had been up all night and desperately needed to sell my fish. On the first take, I was told I was not creepy enough, so on the next take I displayed an Oscar-winning performance of creepiness. However, I grabbed a fake fish to thrust at my customer instead of the real one. Take three. Well, this time I nailed it. It was epic creepiness combined with wild flapping of my dead fish. Given my age and looks, I guess the best I can do is a role as a creepy fish vendor. The stars of the big screen will not have to worry for now.

I hope my friend succeeds with his production company. He did not feel a need to move to Hollywood or New York to accomplish what he believed he was called to do. He chose to grow where he was planted.

It is too easy to compare ourselves to others. When we do, we often come up short. After I ran my first marathon in Chicago, I proudly wore my shirt from the event on the beach while vacationing in Florida. A man approached me and pointed to my shirt saying, "I see you ran the Chicago Marathon." "Yes, I did," I said beaming with pride. He replied, "I run marathons myself. My training partner is Bill Rogers." Bill Rogers happened to be one of America's elite marathoners at that time. "What do you run a marathon in?" I asked him as a matter of curiosity, since I knew who Bill Rogers was. My new acquaintance then drove the final stake into my heart. "Around a 2:20," he stated matter-of-factly. That was almost two hours faster than I had completed my race. Our conversation ended, and I continued my walk down the beach.

You would think I might have learned a lesson after that incident. After completing the Louisville Ironman competition, I was so proud of myself I told everyone the next week about the race. A client called, and I told him what I had done. He told me, "One of my friends did this, too. She finished in eleven hours. How long did the race take you?" I swallowed hard and then said, "I just wanted to complete the race within the time frame. How about those Cincinnati Reds?" I concluded, changing the subject.

You will always find someone who is faster, smarter, better looking or who simply has something that you don't have. Do not let yourself be envious, but rather be comfortable in your own skin. The key in all this is to do the best you can with the talents and abilities you have been given.

ALL IN

CHAPTER NINETEEN

**IRONMAN: TWO HOURS AND FORTY-FIVE MINUTES
UNTIL MIDNIGHT**

The cruelest part of the run is at mile fourteen, which is the turnaround for the run. The crowds are heavier, and I can hear them cheering, "You are almost there. Keep it up." For the faster runners, that is true. However, I still have another lap to go. I can see the finish line just several hundred yards ahead, and then I see the arrow pointing to the second lap. I stop under a light to look at my watch. It is now 9:15. I am just ten minutes ahead of the cut-off time for the second lap, and I have to complete the next 12.2 miles in two and three-quarters hours. To do this, I will have to average 13.5 minutes per mile for the balance of the race. My pace through the first fourteen miles was fifteen minutes per mile. At this rate, I will not make it to the finish before midnight. I have to run the second half of the race faster than the first half. In other words, I have to do a "negative split" in the marathon after swimming 2.4 miles and biking 112 miles. This is something that just doesn't happen.

It is now dark, and I can no longer see my watch. Instead of looking at my watch and running for four minutes and walking for a minute, I have to estimate time by landmarks, which could be a tree or stop light. I run toward the landmark and then walk for a bit.

I catch up with another competitor, and we start talking. We agree to run together for a while. I tell him I plan on running to a landmark and then walking a little. He agrees to try this. This works well for several miles, as I can feel us helping each other. He then begins to tire and says, "This is like the Bataan Death March," before he catches himself. He realizes that negative thoughts should not be introduced. We signed up for the race. No one forced us to be here. This is what we wanted to do. After a bit more running, I begin to feel that if I remain with him I will not finish the race by midnight. He tells me to continue without him, so I go on ahead. Between mile 15.3 and mile 20.1 my pace is 14.30 per mile, which still will not get me to the finish line in time. I am behind and have to pick up the pace even more. When I hit the twenty-mile mark and have just 6.2 miles to go, I give it all I have. I run all I can before exhaustion compels me to stop, and I am forced to take a walking break.

By this time my family is deeply concerned. The window to complete the race in time is closing. A race official asks Stu, "Do you still have your bike?" Stu says he does not. "Well, you had better go looking for him, because it gets lonely out there." Stu and Emily race to look for me. They finally find me a little past the twenty-five-mile marker. My pace from mile 20.1 to 25 has dropped to thirteen minutes per mile. I still have a shot at making it to the finish before midnight. Just as Stu and Emily find me, I stop to throw up. "You can do that later, Dad," Emily says. "You have to just keep pushing. You can do this."

Emily and Stu pace me on the sidewalk, providing encouragement with my every step. Stu then says, "You may think I am your hero, but you are my hero." This barely registers at the time, but it brings tears to my eyes to reflect on it now. Words of encouragement can propel you forward, even when you are running on fumes.

FURTHER REFLECTION

Sometimes you have to give it your all to such an extent you have nothing left at the end. When my son Josh was playing high school basketball, his coach would say, "You have to leave it all on the court." In other words, play your heart out so that you have nothing left to give. Have no regrets when you are finished.

When I was in college, I was recruited by my fraternity for the intramural wrestling team. I weighed less than 140 pounds at that time, and I was good for at least one point by sacrificing myself for the team. Since time was short before my match, I was only taught one move, and that was what to do in the event I was about to be pinned. I happened to draw a high school state champ for my first match. He quickly threw me to the mat and proceeded to pin me. I used that one move three times to avoid being pinned. I somehow survived the first round, but was not so lucky for the next. I was then immediately pinned after my opponent figured out a counter to my move. I felt like a wrung-out dish rag after that match.

More recently, when I studied Tae Kwon Do, we would spar and the matches would last for one minute. That would be the longest minute of my life. You cannot believe how tired you can get with just one minute of all-out fighting. I had to be ALL IN for that minute, or I wouldn't have been able to compete.

END STRONG

CHAPTER TWENTY

IRONMAN: NINETEEN MINUTES UNTIL MIDNIGHT

I pass the twenty-five-mile mark with just nineteen minutes until midnight. I have to cover 1.2 miles in that time. If I can hold a fifteen-minute-per-mile pace and add another three to five minutes for the last two tenths of a mile, I have a window of maybe two minutes to complete the race by midnight. Emily and Stu keep shouting encouragement. "Come on! You are almost there. Just several blocks to go." I turn a corner and then another corner and see the finish line ahead. I thought the only people who would be there were the street sweepers. How wrong I was!

The place is hopping. Screaming crowds line both sides of the street, cheering the last finishers. Many who have completed the race earlier have stayed to cheer their fellow athletes. It is electric. It sends chills through me. I summon my last bit of energy for the conclusion of the race. For the final two blocks of the race, the crowd is packed by the side of the road. I draw energy from the crowd and just keep moving as I approach the finish line. Several yards before the finish I pumped my fist in celebration.

The announcer says, "Doug Thomson, you are an Ironman," as I cross the finish line. My race has been completed in 16 hours, 19 minutes and 39 seconds. I ran the last 1.2 miles at a pace of 12.41 minutes per mile, which was my fastest mile of the race. As it turns out, I complete the race with five and one half minutes to spare. The great irony of the day is that I am significantly under the seventeen hours required to finish the Ironman but almost was not a finisher because of my late swim start.

One of the advantages of being one of the last to finish the Ironman is that I make it into a video of the race. The video is of the last six minutes of the race. I cross the finish line at 16 hours 54 minutes and 19 seconds. I am in better shape than some. Two runners collapse at this finish line. One runner crosses the line and is congratulated by a race volunteer. As the volunteer turns his back to assist another finisher, this runner collapses to the ground. The race volunteer assists him to his feet, supports him with his arm, and walks this dazed and confused finisher off the course. There is a woman finisher who keeps running after she finishes, not realizing she has crossed the line, and has to be stopped. When she realizes she has crossed the finish line, she too collapses, and the video shows four men hauling her off the course to get medical attention. I do not think any of these finishers could have run one more step. In fact I admire these runners even more than

I admire the winner of the race. They were on the course struggling and sweating twice as long as the winner was. You can see their agony and relief as they realize they have made it before the midnight deadline.

FURTHER REFLECTION

With the passage of time, I am spending more time contemplating how I want to run the remainder of my life. My conclusion is that I want to finish strong. If you examine the lives of many men, they have fallen short in the second half of their lives. Consider King Solomon, who was counted among the wisest men who ever lived. While he constructed the Temple and amassed untold riches and fame, it was in the second half of his life that he turned from God. He married over a thousand women and had multiple concubines. What was he thinking? I can imagine some of his conversations with his wives:

"Dear, you forgot our anniversary again!"

"Sorry, I was celebrating my anniversary with two of my other wives that day."

One of the great paradoxes in life is that after working so hard and reaching the pinnacle of success, people often just throw it all away with some fleeting, foolish act. That reminds me of one of my high school basketball coaches, who was known to comment after we squandered a big lead, "You guys just cannot stand prosperity."

You do not have to look far before you see countless modern examples of men falling. A gifted pastor at our old church had an affair and lost his position as pastor of a regional church. The same thing happened at a large church in Colorado Springs. There are countless politicians who have fallen. Some have fallen and, despite this, currently earn hundreds of thousands of dollars in speaking fees. Even though they have survived this, their continued success does not make their behavior right.

The other day, I attended the funeral of a friend who died all too young at the age of forty-nine. When you attend a funeral, you tend to become reflective. As I listened to family and friends describe his life, I was struck not so much by what was said, but rather by what was not said. Rather than listing his accomplishments, all spoke of who he was. They spoke of his love for his family and his desire to stay involved in their lives. One of his sisters had lost her husband, so my friend had stepped in to be a surrogate father to their children. All this occurred while he was trying to be a good husband and father to his own four children. One of his children had special needs, and he founded a soccer league in Cincinnati to provide an avenue for those physically and mentally challenged children to participate in a sport in a supportive environment. Accomplishments are soon forgotten, but investments in the lives of others will live on.

At the conclusion of my life, I want it said of me that I loved God, was faithful to my wife and honored my marital vows, was a good father to my children, was honest in business and fair in my dealings with others, and attempted to live by the golden rule.

I want to finish well and hear the host of heaven cheering me as I cross the finish line. I want to hear the words of Jesus, as he greets me and I collapse in his arms from exhaustion, "Well done, my good and faithful servant." While it is unlikely that the world will ever hear of me, I want to play the game truly and do the best I can to do right and to treat people with respect and honesty.

I recently read an article in Sports Illustrated about the second running revolution in the United States. The author was describing a man in his eighties who had just won a race in his age group; he was smiling and giving everyone high fives and then he took several steps past the finish line, collapsed and died. The author commented, "This is not a bad exit strategy." I agree. End strong doing what you enjoy. That is how I want to end.

LESSONS FROM THE FINISH

CHAPTER TWENTY-ONE

IRONMAN: POST RACE

After I cross the finish line, I am handed a Finisher's Medal by the race winner, along with a hat and a shirt. I wave to Gretchen, Emily and Stu. Barbara has had to leave early with Sam because he has school the next day, so they are not there for the finish. I want to go over to my family to talk, but after I walk for several steps, I proceed to get sick. A volunteer helps me to a chair and scoots a trash barrel over to me, and I empty the contents of my stomach into it. I am sure this is truly a lovely spectacle for the race officials to witness.

After several minutes, a volunteer asks if I am all right. I say, "I am feeling light-headed and dehydrated." He says he had better summon a wheelchair. A wheelchair is found for me and the volunteer begins to briskly wheel me out of the finish area. After a minute or so of brisk walking I ask, "Where are you taking me?"

LESSONS FROM THE FINISH

"Wherever you want," is his response.

"I want to go back to my family," I reply. He then does an abrupt about-face, nearly spilling me out of the wheelchair, and we head back to the finish line. We find Gretchen, Emily and Stu and they ask, "What are you doing back here? You need to be checked out." Again the volunteer does an abrupt about-face, and we head to the medical area. This time Stu accompanies me.

We enter the medical area and it looks like a war zone from MASH. The cots are filled with runners in various degrees of pain. They locate an empty cot, and I collapse into it. It feels good to stop moving. My blood pressure is taken. It is 170 over 110, which I am told is good. It is determined that I do not need an I.V. I am given some chicken broth instead. The man next to me is not so lucky. He has an I.V. and is covered with blankets. Despite this, he is shaking uncontrollably. I think they eventually took him to the hospital.

After resting for several more minutes, I am ready to be released, and the doctor discharges me. Stu helps me get up, as I am stiff by this time. He helps me hobble across the street to the hotel and up to our room. My focus now is on a hot bath and then bed.

FURTHER REFLECTION

After finishing the race I reflect back on some of the lessons that I have learned. Here are a few:

Be Focused

To find the time to train for the Ironman, I had to set aside virtually all my outside activities for one year and focus on this event. It is easy to be drawn into other commitments, but to train for an event of this magnitude requires incredible focus. My wife commented to me during the course of the year, "All you do is work, train and sleep." Yes, that sums it up. The training built up to twenty hours in one week, and once you factor in a work week often in excess of fifty hours, that does not leave much time for anything else.

Prior to training for the Ironman, I worked to get my black belt in Tae Kwon Do. One of the tests for the black belt was to break a concrete block with my bare hand. The block was about one inch thick. It is easy to be intimidated by this requirement. The natural tendency is to pull your punch so that you stop as you hit the block. To be successful in breaking the concrete block, you have to focus on a point about one to two inches behind the block and hit the block with the edge of your hand. You do not get a chance to practice on a block before the test.

When it was time for the test, the block was set on two cinder blocks, and I began to focus. I thought, "There is no way I am *not* going to break this block with all these people watching. I would rather break my hand first!" I nearly got my wish. I hit the block as hard as I could and let out a convincing karate yell. The side of my arm also hit the block at the same time my hand did. The block broke and fell between the cinder blocks, and everyone clapped at my success. At the time I did not realize that the strike had bruised the edge of my arm. The next week it turned an ugly shade of black, but it eventually healed.

With concentration and focused attention, there is no limit to what you can accomplish. You have to be willing to pay the price of focus. Along with the focusing comes a weighing of life's priorities and elimination of those activities which do not move you closer toward your goal.

Run Your Race with Integrity

Unlike the Tour de France, where drafting is permitted, the bike portion of the Ironman is an individual effort. When you are passing someone, you have fifteen seconds to complete the pass. If you are being passed, you are to fall back four bike lengths behind the individual who passed you. Although while I am in training I ride by myself, on the few occasions when I have ridden in a group, I have learned that drafting makes a huge difference. You can go several miles per hour faster with drafting, and over 112 miles, this difference is monumental in terms of time. In fact, they have individuals on motorcycles patrolling the course to make sure someone does not violate the rules. If you break the rules and draft, you have to spend five minutes in the penalty tent. At two infractions, you are disqualified and have to call it an early day. Fortunately, during the course of the race, I did not see anyone in any of the penalty tents.

While the discussion in this chapter may seem obvious, it is more important today than ever. My son Josh was accepted as a cadet to the United States Air Force Academy. When we were visiting the Academy for orientation, etched in stone above a walkway is the honor code for the Academy. When the cadets are admitted to the program they take an oath to abide by the code. The code is simple, and it can be easily committed to memory. It says simply, "We will not lie, steal, or cheat, nor tolerate among us anyone who does." The honor code could have contained a number of things, such as I agree to turn in all my homework on time. Instead, it was reduced to agreeing not to lie, steal or cheat and to purge from the ranks anyone who does. Why is this so important?

Several years ago I completed a leadership program called "Clermont 2020". Since I am now an alumnus of that program, I volunteered to help the incoming class with planning for their assigned day. I decided to throw out an idea. I began by saying, "I think a major problem today is 'whom can you trust?' It seems that everywhere you turn, people are either cutting corners or violating some trust. You have financial advisors stealing their customers' money, football coaches covering up disgusting behavior by their assistants, baseball players who cork their bats to hit more home runs and athletes who use performance-enhancing drugs. Just whom can you trust now? We need to do our seminar on integrity. If you cannot trust anyone, here is what happens. People turn inward and keep their money close to their chests. The only way we can turn this around is if we mobilize a grass roots effort to lead lives of integrity. Perhaps people will be inspired by what we do and follow our example." Surprisingly, the group agreed with the suggestion and began to plan the day's events around integrity.

History abounds with famous cheaters. I remember watching the New York Marathon one year. There was a lady who ran several miles and then jumped onto the subway and rode around under the city for a while. She then popped up and exited a station ahead of the leader. She ran the last several miles to the thunderous applause of the crowd. When she finished, the race officials were perplexed. None of the leaders had seen her pass them. "How did she get so far ahead?" they wondered. They also wondered why her shirt was not even wet. The officials finally figured out what happened, and she was disqualified.

If everyone cheats, no one really wins. Cheating just causes the social fabric to erode thread by thread.

Here is what happens: with cheating comes the loss of integrity. If someone is caught lying or cheating, it may take years to restore trust. You are always wondering in the back of your mind, "Can I trust this person?" Consequently, you are always on your guard.

With the loss of trust comes the loss of respect. With the loss of respect comes the loss of moral authority. With the loss of moral authority comes the inability to be taken seriously. Finally, and most fatal of all, is the loss of legitimacy.

It is nearly impossible not to notice the decline in moral behavior today. The only way to turn around the erosion of the social fabric is to run the race that is set before you with integrity. Be an example. Be a light to others and refuse to cut corners. Run the race set before you with integrity, and you will make a difference.

Family Support

As you push toward the finish of any great undertaking you need to reflect on those who helped get you there. The Apollo mission to put a man on the moon required the concentration and dedication of thousands, and yet only one person, Neil Armstrong, was the first to actually set foot on the moon. If you read about expeditions to scale Mt. Everest, this requires a large staff to support the few who attack the summit. The same can be said for the Ironman competition.

Training for an Ironman takes a tremendous toll on the family. I work fifty to sixty hours per week at my job, and trying to squeeze in training on top of a long work week was incredibly difficult. While I could get up early to do my swim and run, I would often ride my bike in the evening after dinner. This did not leave much family time. Weekends were even worse. I would schedule a long bike ride on Saturdays and a long run on Sundays. After building up my bike ride to over 100 miles on Saturday, I found that

I was exhausted most of the day. Once I returned home, I did not feel like doing much other than lying on the couch and contemplating the long run I would need to do on Sunday. After running for three or more hours on Sunday, I was useless for the rest of the weekend.

Fortunately, my wife understood, and she supported me in my quest. I know that other families experience the same thing. I saw one lady at the Ironman who was wearing a t-shirt that said, "140.6 miles until I get my husband back."

Because of the time commitment, and in fairness to my family, this is not the kind of sacrifice I want to repeat. However, for some families, this is not a sacrifice. It is a lifestyle. There were many couples I saw who travel around the country competing in Ironman competitions. They were young and apparently did not have children. You get to see great areas of the nation and be ultra-fit in the process. It is easy to get caught up in hyper-competitiveness. If you are competitive, you are always looking for ways to improve and find that secret method of training or nutrition to give you the edge.

On the way up to our hotel room, my wife overheard a conversation between two other wives. One said to the other, as if to proclaim it as a badge of honor, "My husband will only drink bottled water." On the other hand, I drink water wherever it may be found. I do not think whether my water is bottled or from the faucet that it will have an appreciable impact on my performance. There is a time and place for everything. I needed the support of my family without going overboard.

Without the support of my family, my training would have been unbearable. As it says in scripture, "A house divided against itself cannot stand" (Matthew 12:25). The same can be said of training for the race. Unless you have family support for this daunting task, attempting an Ironman will only hurt and divide your family. You need to obtain complete buy-in from the family. Your family needs to recognize that as you approach the race, you will become increasingly grumpy and useless. They need to love you anyway.

During the race, the support of my family made all the difference. One of the greatest moments of my life was when Stu and Emily were running beside me the last half mile of the race, offering encouragement as I approached the finish line. That is a moment that is etched in the core of my being. I could not have completed the race without their support.

Sometimes family support comes from just being together and enjoying each other's company. Stu enjoys cooking. He has watched the Cooking Channel several times and is now a self-proclaimed expert. One day he observed me making a peanut butter and jelly sandwich. He saw me spread the peanut butter and then the jelly and offered the following advice, "You are using too much jelly. It will spill out the sides." I replied, "I am 60 years old and you would think by now I can make a peanut butter and jelly sandwich. Besides, I like my sandwich with a lot of jelly," I replied, heaping on extra jelly for emphasis.

"You are still using too much," Stu said ending our conversation.

Stu enjoys giving advice, even to those who do not care to receive it. One day my daughter Emily joined us for a bike ride. She doesn't ride much and is somewhat of a novice, although she would vehemently disagree with that assessment. I looked back and saw Stu instructing Emily on the proper technique to drink from her water bottle while riding. Emily was frowning, and I am not sure whether it was from the exertion or Stu's instruction. Stu was holding the water bottle to the side and happily squirting the water into his mouth as he rides. He continued his cheerful patter: "You drink like this. You hold the bottle to the side so you can see where you ride."

Following the episodes with the peanut butter and jelly sandwich and Stu's instructions to Emily, we thought of conspiring against Stu. Attending Emily's church was a gifted athlete by the name of Jamie Smith, who is from Australia. He was training to try out for the Australian Olympic team as a marathon runner, but due to an injury had to abandon his dream of running in the Olympics and now focuses on his bike riding. He is incredibly fast, and one time he rode from Cincinnati to Cleveland averaging over twenty miles per hour by himself and without drafting. His personality closely resembles the self-assured and swashbuckling Aussie "Crocodile Dundee" from the movie. He doesn't take any grief from anybody. We thought it would be great sport to pair Jamie with Stu. We would explain to Stu. "Jamie is a rookie rider who desperately needs instruction on the basics of bike riding and on the fine art of drinking from his water bottle. Do you think you can help our friend?" We would then turn Stu loose on the unsuspecting Jamie and step back and watch the fireworks. You, dear reader, are sworn to secrecy as we try to initiate our plot. Family support may even take the form of pranks, which can add spice to life.

Sometimes family support is just being there in a time of need. Following his bone marrow transplant, Stu's brother Steve, who is a medical doctor, needed some financial help. He had just graduated from medical school, had a young family and plenty of bills from school loans. He asked Stu for some money. Stu at this time was just starting out financially and did not have a great deal of financial reserves. As Stu was contemplating his request, we could not help but wade in with unsolicited advice of our own. We said, "Stu, do you think that Steve will remember you when he pays his debts off and is driving around town in his Lamborghini?" Stu brushed off our comments and said simply, "He is my brother, and I want to help." That was his decision and the end of our discussion. That is the essence of family support and why I so appreciated Stu's support during the race.

Seize the Day

How often do we see an athlete or performer who seems to come out of nowhere to rise to the top, and we and think, "That person is an overnight success." What we do not realize is that behind that overnight success is someone who has devoted hours of practice to their profession or craft. I once had the opportunity to hear Dr. Robert D. Ballard speak. He is most noted for the discoveries of the wrecks of the RMS *Titanic* in 1985, the battleship *Bismarck* in 1989, and the aircraft carrier USS *Yorktown* in 1998. He also discovered the wreck of John F. Kennedy's PT-109. He said one thing in particular that made an impression and stuck with me. He said, "People often come up to me and say, 'I want to be just like you.'" I reply, "To be just like me will require a PhD in marine geology and geophysics and many other advanced degrees in other disciplines. After that comes years of work." Just listing his degrees shows the amount of effort he put in to get where he is. In 1965, Ballard graduated from the University of California, Santa Barbara, earning undergraduate degrees in chemistry and geology. His first graduate degree (MS, 1966) was in geophysics from the University of Hawaii's Institute of Geophysics, where he trained porpoises and whales. After that, he received a PhD in marine geology and geophysics at the University of Rhode Island. Years of work combined with focus and determination allowed Ballard to seize opportunity when it was presented.

I watched a documentary video of pianists who were training for a national amateur piano competition. Now that I am beginning to teach myself piano, I have a greater appreciation for what they have accomplished. Several of the competitors were featured in the documentary. One was a physician who practiced for up to five hours per day. How he found the time to practice with a demanding schedule and with a family is amazing enough. I have trouble concentrating for the thirty minutes I practice per day. He somehow maintained his focus and concentration for five hours. To compete in the competition he had to memorize pages of music which contained hundreds of difficult notes. After all this time of practice, he was rewarded with a victory in the competition.

For him to seize the day, he had to practice most of the day. Ability combined with practice gives the victory.

Enjoy the View

For Stu, the positive outcome from his illness has been that he has learned to treasure life. He makes each day count and lives life to the fullest by squeezing out everything he can. Here are a couple of Stu stories which reveal his character. Stu came for a visit over Father's Day weekend to help me with my training. I was invited by one of my Masters Swim Team teammates to an event called "Eat, Ride, and Eat," and Stu was invited to come along. We were treated to a wonderful breakfast, which was to be followed by a fifty-mile bike ride, and then the day would conclude with a lunch feast.

Our journey began when we headed west from our host's house on Eastern Avenue and continued past the Reds' and Bengals' stadiums. As often happens, the faster riders picked up the pace, and our group began to spread out. I struggled to keep near the front. As we were crossing the 8th Street Viaduct, which always seems to be in a state of repair (or disrepair, depending on how you look at it), I heard the cry of "Biker down!" This alarm is never good, and it was especially unwelcome in this section of road. Fortunately, we were riding early when the traffic was light, but soon cement trucks and semis would come barreling down this stretch as they made haste to deliver their loads. It would be difficult for these trucks to stop in time to avoid a biker planted in the middle of the street.

I looked behind us and saw one of our group sprawled in the middle of the road. People were rushing to her aid. Stu had already turned around and was dismounting to give assistance. He jostled her stunned companion aside. We later found out that was her husband.

Stu sprang into action and began to ask her questions to see if she had a concussion. Stu had suffered a concussion in a biking accident, so he knew what to look for. While Stu is not a doctor, his brother is. Furthermore, Stu had watched a few episodes of *General Hospital* when he was growing up, so armed with these solid credentials Stu began to render assistance. He began his medical evaluation by firing her some basic questions in rapid succession. "Who is the prime minister of Italy, what is the eighth digit of pi, and who was Eisenhower's Secretary of State?" Stu asked while impatiently anticipating a reply.

"Oh, my aching head," she moaned over and over as she held her head. Her current distress was not so much due to her head injury as to trying to process Stu's staccato delivery of questioning. These questions were followed by some easier questions, and while it was determined she was banged up, it did not look as if she had a head injury. "She will be fine," was Stu's concluding diagnosis. We later found out that the man Stu pushed aside was not only her husband but was one of Cincinnati's foremost children's oncology specialists. I suspect somewhere along the line he was qualified to treat her injury. We summoned help, and her husband remained with her until help arrived. We also found out this was their anniversary. That is an anniversary they will always remember. The story has a happy ending. Fortunately, after she had received treatment, they were able to join us later that evening.

While certain aspects of this tale have been embellished, there are certain undeniable truths. Know this. Stu is a take-charge kind of guy, and even if you are Cincinnati's foremost doctor in your field, that will not help you when Stu springs into action. He will move heaven and earth to provide assistance. He has compassion and will go to great lengths to help the fallen. It is no wonder that I dedicated my race to him.

Several years ago, Stu and his family were invited to attend Camp Highlands, which is one of the oldest family camps in the United States. Our family was also invited to attend. One of my memories of the camp was of a mounted moose. The daily menu was hung from the mouth of this poor defunct creature.

Prior to Stu's arrival, the camping families had enjoyed a peaceful week, lounging by the lake, leisurely paddling in a canoe or just simply enjoying listening to haunting morning cry of the loon. After all, vacationing is for relaxing, right? That all changed with the arrival of Stu. Not content to sit still for one minute, Stu believed that all the other campers should have a major dose of hyperactivity. Stu organized running events, canoe races, sailboat marathons, and basically drove the other campers to a mind-numbing stupor of exhaustion by the end of each day. I remember one episode in which he induced a bunch of us to swim across the lake. After battling the freezing water and waves, we finally made it to the other side, only to be greeted by a host committee of mosquitoes and swarming black flies. There is one problem with swimming across a lake. You have to swim back.

The next day I went camping with Stu and our sons. We paddled across the lake to an island. Stu's friends were glad to see us leave, and quickly arranged a golf game for early the next morning. We had a great time setting up our tents and settling in for the night. Early the next morning, Stu had to go to the bathroom, and since the island where we were camping did not have any facilities, Stu decided to paddle his canoe across the lake and use the facilities at the camp. Just as he was arriving at the camp, his friends were leaving to play golf. Their car was parked so that the headlights shone onto the lake. One of the golfers said, "Look, do you see something out on the lake?"

"What is that?" another golfer asked.

"I think it is someone in a canoe. Who would ever be paddling a canoe at this hour of the morning? What sort of maniac would be canoeing this early?" they asked, in disbelief that someone would actually be on the lake.

Just then the figure got close enough to be identified. "It's Stu!" they all cried in unison. "Doesn't that guy ever rest?" someone asked. in exasperated envy at his stamina. They quickly left for their golf game before Stu had a chance to arrange another canoe race.

When my two eldest children were young, we would often make a trip to the Great Smoky Mountains. One fall day, we decided to take a hike. Taking our day hiking gear, we began our trek. The trail wound for miles up the mountain and was covered with a canopy of trees. Suddenly the trail opened onto a field, which is something unusual in the Smoky Mountains. We stopped and decided to take a rest.

Since this was the fall and we were high in the mountains, the air was chilly, but because there were few clouds to interrupt the sunlight, the temperature of the air at ground level was warm. We took off our jackets and took a nap in the field. The meadow overlooked a spacious valley below, and I just savored the warm feel of the field, the wildflowers and the view.

When we made our trip to the Smokies, we stayed high in the mountains. Our unit was near the crest of the mountain. One evening it rained hard, and we could hear the storm rolling in. When we went on our balcony to look outside, we realized we were watching a thunderstorm from above the clouds. We could see the lightning jump out of the clouds.

Sometimes you just have to savor the view and enjoy the experience. During the Ironman race, I tried to savor the moment even if it was painful. I savored the climb on the bike and the burning in my legs as I slowly pedaled the hills. I savored the feeling of accomplishment when I made it to the top of a hill. I savored the downhill portion of the course when I could rest. I savored seeing my family there to encourage me.

Do not feel like you have to rush through the moment, but take your time to enjoy it and savor the view.

I think back often to the day of the race, and I still wonder how I made it. I savored every moment of the adventure: the training, the experience of getting stronger and better, the words of encouragement from my daughter and Stu as I neared the finish line, and the thrill of crossing the finish line under the time limit. These are moments I will always treasure and savor.

I find it difficult to slow down. Sometimes I feel like a spring that is coiled and ready to snap. Several years ago I promised my wife a weekend at French Lick, Indiana. Due to the busyness of life, I was not able to deliver until recently. It was worth the wait. One of the restored resorts in the town, West Baden, enjoyed considerable acclaim during the Roaring Twenties. It features an enormous rotunda which is the largest of its type in the United States. This area is renowned for its mineral springs, and many people come to bathe and drink the mineral waters. My wife and I decided to end our visit with a mineral bath. When I checked into the spa, I was given these instructions: "After you change, put on the bathrobe in your locker and head down the hall to the waiting room, where you will find refreshments and relaxing music." I was handed a key and looked forward to my time of pampering and soaking in the large tub. After I entered the locker room, I found my locker and inserted the key. I turned the key and found that the locker was locked. I was annoyed. I had not considered that the locker might be unlocked when I first inserted the key. I twisted again, trying to force the key into a full circle. As I pushed and twisted I felt the key bending in the lock. I knew that if I kept turning, the key would certainly shear in the lock and I could never get the locker open. I then reversed my turn and was able to extract the key from the lock. I examined it and did not like what I saw. It was not only bent but I had sheared it. The end was dangling, and a small sliver of metal was all that was keeping the end from falling off. I thought the best course of action was to take this to the front desk and try to exchange it for another key.

I approached the friendly clerk and she smiled, no doubt wondering why I was still in my street clothes. I decided the best course of action was to utter a simple declaratory sentence. "Your key is broken," I said, without revealing the source of the damage, and handed her the mangled key. Her eyes then widened, and I could tell that she was thinking, "What in the world has this guy done with my key? He has destroyed it in just a few moments. If he can create that much damage trying to open a locker, I can just imagine what he will do with the rest of the spa. I better sign him up for an extended session if he is under that much stress." She was too polite to speak what she was thinking, as she handed me another key and said, "We will take care of the key, sir." I did manage to take my mineral bath without further incident, and I was able to enjoy some untroubled time savoring the experience.

Often we spend so much time planning for the future that we do not live in and appreciate the moment. Here is a story about enjoying what you have.

An American tourist was at the pier of a small coastal Mexican village when a small boat with just one fisherman docked. Inside the small boat were several large yellowfin tuna. The tourist complimented the Mexican on the quality of his fish and asked how long it took to catch them.

The Mexican replied, "Only a little while."

The tourist then asked, "Why didn't you stay out longer and catch more fish?" The Mexican said, "With this I have more than enough to support my family's needs."

The tourist then asked, "But what do you do with the rest of your time?"

The Mexican fisherman said, "I sleep late, fish a little, play with my children, take siesta with my wife, Maria, stroll into the village each evening where I sip wine and play guitar with my amigos. I have a full and busy life."

The tourist scoffed, "I can help you. You should spend more time fishing and with the proceeds, buy a bigger boat. With the proceeds from the bigger boat you could buy several boats. Eventually you would have a fleet of fishing boats. Instead of selling your catch to a middleman you would sell directly to the processor; eventually opening your own cannery. You would control the product, processing and distribution. You could leave this small coastal fishing village and move to Mexico City, then Los Angeles and eventually New York where you could run your ever-expanding enterprise."

The Mexican fisherman asked, "But, how long will this all take?"

The tourist replied, "Fifteen to twenty years."

"But what then?" asked the Mexican.

The tourist laughed and said, "That's the best part. When the time is right you would sell your company stock to the public and become very rich. You would make millions."

"Millions? Then what?"

The American said, "Then you would retire. Move to a small coastal fishing village where you would sleep late, fish a little, play with your kids, take siesta with your wife, stroll to the village in the evenings where you could sip wine and play your guitar with your amigos."

Not all views are good views, but you have to figure out a way to enjoy them no matter what. There is a story about a man who took his family to the east coast to experience the Atlantic Ocean. He saw a sign at a hotel which said, "Ocean View". Based on that promise he checked into the hotel and after locating their room, he discovered it was located on the backside of the building overlooking a parking lot and not the ocean. He went down to the front desk to complain. "I thought you said the room had an ocean view," he stated.

The clerk looked up and answered, "I did, but I did not say which ocean."

Sometimes life gives us the keys to a view that is not our choosing. Recently I visited my dad at his retirement home in Florida. When we were eating lunch with a group of his friends, I noticed a man at the next table laughing, telling jokes and just having a good time. He then proceeded to engage our table in conversation. Despite being hooked up to several tubes of oxygen to help him with his breathing, he still managed to enjoy life. One of the people at a nearby table leaned over and commented, "Everyone enjoys being with him. He is so much fun." I sincerely hope that when I am his age I can look at the bright side and enjoy the view I have been given.

There is a season in life for everything. One of my friends was a gifted high school and college athlete. I asked him why he was not continuing to compete. He responded, "I remember my times in high school and in college. If I were to compete now, my times would be much slower and it would just kill me not to be able to perform as fast." That may be true, but you can still enjoy doing all you can in the present. I will continue to swim as long as I can in the master's program. How long I can continue I do not know, because many of the swimmers are twenty or even thirty years younger than I am.

The time will come, however, when I can no longer

keep up. At that time, I hope I have the grace to switch to something different, such as sailing, where I can let the wind do the work. Who knows? I may try to be competitive in the sport and see how far I can get. Wouldn't it be something to make the Olympic team? You can never stop hoping and dreaming. The key is to enjoy the season, to enjoy whatever view you have been given at the moment.

FINAL THOUGHTS

CHAPTER TWENTY-TWO

FURTHER REFLECTION

What an odyssey this has been! There are two components to all this. First, you have to get to the race, and then you have to get through the race. As I reflect back, I survived a number of falls on my bike. I could have been injured on any one of these and would have had to abandon training. I trained in the freezing rain. I trained in the brutal sun. I trained when I did not feel like training, but still I trained, because I had a goal and purpose in mind. My bike had multiple failures just several weeks before the race. If I had any equipment failures during the race, I could not have recovered. I reduced the time needed to change my tire from an hour when my swim coach helped rescue me on the Loveland Bike Trail to fifteen minutes. I practiced this drill and was prepared, but with even one flat tire, I would not have been able to complete the race in time. During this year, I did not get injured and only got sick once. Any illness could have set back my training schedule.

Yes, everything had to come together to allow me to

finish within the required time. It did. Could I have gone faster? After every race you can think of ways to improve. I could have cut time by hustling more at the transition area and not dallying at the bike rest stops. I could have focused more on my time in the bike segment rather than on my heart rate, but I question whether I might have been one of those lying prostrate by the side of the road. I did what I needed to do. I accomplished my goal, which was to complete an Ironman within the allotted time, without injury and in good shape. I ended up placing 41st in my division and 2108 overall out of the 3050 who were registered. Particularly indicative of the impact the ninety-three-degree heat had that day was the fact that approximately half of the competitors in my age group did not finish the race. I count myself fortunate to be an Ironman finisher. I met my goal and am satisfied with that.

All this could not have been accomplished without the support of my family. Competing in an Ironman is incredibly stressful, not only for the athlete but for the whole family as well. Hours from home are spent in training. After a long bike ride or run, I am tired and grumpy and frankly just feel like lying around for the rest of the day. I want to thank my wife Gretchen for allowing me to pursue this dream. Her support means more than she will ever know. Stu has been an inspiration in my life for his courage in dealing with a life-threatening illness. My daughter Emily was there during the tough moments of the race, providing words of encouragement. Sam and Barbara cheered during the race. Many friends tracked my progress and were praying during the course of the race. Truly, completing an Ironman was one of the great highlights of my life. Now it is on to activities that are a little less stressful, such as playing the piano.

My final thoughts center on our Creator, without whose provision and care I could never have completed the race. There were just too many things that could have gone wrong but did not. My bike chain could have broken during the race. I had just gotten a new chain installed on my bike at the beginning of the season, and yet it broke just several weeks before the race. Stu and Emily showed up just at the right time to provide words of encouragement during the race. Yes, God's provision and care were evident throughout. To His name be the glory and thanks. Amen and Amen.

I received this post from my daughter on my website, and it brings tears to my eyes to recall it. "There are moments in life that stand still allowing you to truly soak up the significance. Running on the sidelines while Stu ran next to you yelling encouragement during your last mile of the race was one of those moments for me. When you rounded the last corner and headed towards the finish I had to start dodging the roaring crowd in order to stay with you, but for just a moment it was as if everyone was quiet, the music stopped, and all I could hear was Stu yelling to you, 'Doug, you think I am your hero?! You are my hero—you are an Ironman!' I took a picture of that moment in my mind and will never forget. You are both my heroes. I am very proud of you. Love you Dad!"

MATTHEW 25: MINISTRIES

Matthew 25: Ministries will receive all proceeds from this book. If you have received any value from reading it, please consider a donation to this ministry. I have been involved as a director since the ministry began. A number of years ago, I had the opportunity to participate in a mission trip and view at the ground level the impact of this ministry. We were scheduled to go to Nicaragua just after their civil war had ended. As may be expected, the country was devastated, and medical supplies and attention were in short supply.

I remember flying into the airport in the capital city of Managua. There were still anti aircraft guns guarding the field and men with weapons everywhere. Our mission for the trip was to help set up a neonatal care unit at the local children's hospital. At the time, I was working part-time as counsel to a medical group, and I invited one of my friends, Dan, to go with me. For some reason, I could not go on the flight with him but planned to fly down several days later. Dan called me before I left and commented, "It sure is noisy down here. Roosters are crowing and dogs are barking all through the night. It is hard to sleep."

On our first visit to the hospital to scope out our project, we took some toys to pass out to some of the children in the burn unit. Burns and respiratory issues were common in the country at the time. People would cook over open fires, and children would often fall into the flames. Wood was scarce, and people would burn garbage and particularly plastic as fuel. It would not take many days of inhaling the toxic fumes of burning plastic bags before people would develop respiratory issues.

When we handed out the toys, I noticed that many of the children would not smile or even acknowledge the gift. Dan took me aside and asked as if he read my thoughts, "Do you know why these kids are not smiling?"

"No," I replied.

"The reason these kids are not smiling is because they are in pain. I have checked, and the strongest medication they have is Tylenol. They are in severe pain and that is why they are not smiling." All I could do is nod as what he said sunk in.

That is the purpose of the ministry of Matthew 25. The ministry is in the business of alleviating pain through provision of food, medical supplies, clothing, and other basic necessities. I hope you have the opportunity to learn more and to also become involved. Our journey on this earth is short, and I hope that you will choose to make a difference in the lives of others.

ABOUT THE AUTHOR

Douglas W. Thomson is an attorney and businessman. He has served as counsel to a high technology company, has been Mayor of the City of Milford, Ohio, and has served on the Board of Directors of Matthew 25: Ministries since its inception. He has a wide range of interests, including competing in triathlons, hydroponic gardening, writing and thinking of ways to save the world. His wife, Gretchen, likes to keep him busy so he doesn't become distracted and lead her on another wild adventure. He has three children, Joshua, Emily, and Samuel, and resides in Cincinnati, Ohio.

RACE SPLITS
Swim 1:24 | Bike 8:06 | Run 6:20

DID YOU ENJOY
GIANT JOURNEYS?

Douglas W. Thomson would love to hear from you!

To share your thoughts about this book,
email him at dthomson@cincilaw.com or
visit www.kenwoodpublishinggroup.com.

**Visit the links below for more information
about Matthew 25: Ministries**

www.m25m.org

Facebook.com/m25m.org

Twitter.com/m25m_org

Pinterest.com/m25m

Made in the USA
San Bernardino, CA
06 April 2015